THE SAN FRANCISCO
CENTURY

A CITY RISES

FROM THE RUINS

OF THE 1906

EARTHQUAKE

AND FIRE

THE SAN FRANCISCO
CENTURY

BY CARL NOLTE
AND THE SAN FRANCISCO CHRONICLE STAFF

The San Francisco Chronicle Press

The San Francisco Century

Editor: Narda Zacchino

Senior Editor: Jay Johnson

Art Director: Dorothy A. Yule

Photo Editors: Jim Merithew,
    Susan Gilbert

Photo Researcher: Laura Perkins

Copy Editor: Jennifer Thelen

Imagining Technician:
    Nina Costales

Pre-Press: Brad Zucroff,
    Omnivorous Media

Book Development Director:
    Dickson Louie

The San Francisco Chronicle

Publisher: Frank Vega

Editor: Phil Bronstein

**Page 2: The towering Golden
Gate Bridge is the signature
symbol of San Francisco.**

The San Francisco Chronicle Press

901 Mission Street, San Francisco, CA 94103
www.sfchroniclepress.com

Library of Congress Control Number: 2005927447

ISBN 0-9760880-8-8

Distributed by Sterling Publishing Co., Inc.

Printed and bound in China

First Printing August 2005

Every effort has been made to ensure that the information in this book, including photo credits, is accurate. Any errors or credit omissions are inadvertent, and we apologize for them in advance. Corrections will be published in any future editions.

10   38   58   84

110

C O N T E N T S

136

166

194

224

City of Magic, Century of Change

A boomtown of pioneers, wizards, brigands, and entrepreneurs, San Francisco was already wild and magical on the morning of April 18, 1906. Afterward, with the city left in ruins by the powerful forces of nature, it would have been difficult to imagine that it could ever recover, much less regain its uniquely daring energy. Yet not only was San Francisco rapidly rebuilt, but over the next one hundred years the city itself became a creative force of nature, changing the rest of the world as well as entertaining it. Producing great literature, high-tech inventions, political movements, trend-setting cuisine, and more, the city continues to be a place on the edge — of a continent, a culture, and the imagination. San Francisco also has been an exhilarating place to be both resident and journalist. This book, the work of the staff of the 140-year-old *San Francisco Chronicle*, has been produced with the same passion and affection for the city that San Franciscans have felt since its founding. *The San Francisco Century* shows us why the city is so beloved by natives, transplants, visitors, and the millions who have only seen photographs or heard stories of this jewel of a city.

— *Phil Bronstein, Editor, San Francisco Chronicle*

San Francisco is a city where unusual things are usual — such as a tram car with legs. The one opposite is a Moscow tram, presented to San Francisco in 1987 by the consul general of the former Soviet Union.

Looking into the mirror of the past: San Francisco just after the turn of the twentieth century was a city of light and color and sounds — the clang of cable cars, the clop of horses' hooves on cobblestone and brick streets. San Francisco had tall new buildings and smart shops and stores. Men dressed in dark coats and women in full-length dresses. Even children wore hats. Police officers wore long blue coats and tall helmets. Lotta's Fountain (above) at Market, Kearny and Geary streets was the center of it all, and if you waited there long enough, San Franciscans said, everybody you knew would pass by.

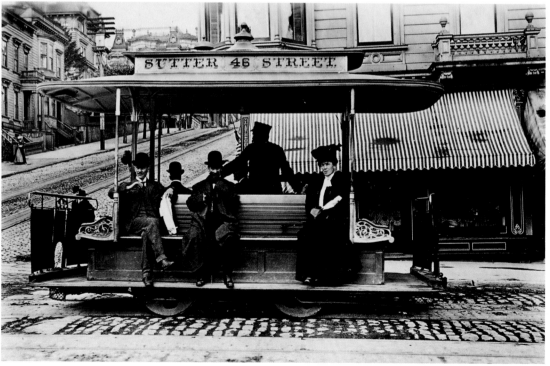

PART ONE

The City That Was

Dazed San Franciscans on Market Street watch flames finish what an earthquake started on April 18, 1906. Pages 12-13: Arnold Genthe's view down Sacramento Street has been called one of the ten best news photographs of all time.

Even a century ago, San Franciscans considered their city a special place. After all, it was the only real city on the western edge of North America: it had a population of four hundred thousand and was so important that one-quarter of the people west of the Rockies lived within fifty miles of San Francisco Bay. It had grown from a sleepy, insignificant Mexican village to the eighth-largest city in the United States in just sixty years and had become the biggest port on the West Coast. It was a manufacturing center and a financial capital, a city whose residents patronized the opera and the theater, a city of writers and artists. It was surrounded on three sides by water, like Constantinople; it was built on hills, like Rome; it was cultured, like Vienna; it was as sinful as Cairo. Tourists compared it to Paris — and to Sodom and Gomorrah.

That old San Francisco died in a catastrophic earthquake and a fire that burned for three days just after Easter 1906.

In the city's wood-frame houses, foundations cracked, plaster crumbled, and walls and floors buckled. Many people were killed at home when brick chimneys crashed through roofs. Opposite: Six hours after the last performance at the Majestic Theater on Market Street, the roof fell in. Fire soon destroyed what remained. Pages 16-17: A crowd gathers in front of a collapsed row of wood-frame flats on Golden Gate Avenue near Hyde Street as smoke and fire loom in the background on the morning of the quake. The entire area burned later in the day.

When the disaster was over, Sydney Tyler, a war correspondent and author, wrote it had left the city "a blackened, ruined thing, the pity of the world." In New York, journalist Will Irwin wrote the obituary of San Francisco, which he called "The City That Was." But the symbol on the official seal of the City and County of San Francisco is the phoenix, the legendary bird that is destroyed by fire only to rise from its own ashes. And in San Francisco that terrible spring, some of the survivors, as they liked to call themselves, recited a poem by Larry Harris that began:

> From the Ferries to Van Ness
>
> You're a God-forsaken mess,
>
> But the damndest finest ruins —
>
> Nothin' more or nothin' less.

How the city rose from the ruins and became the San Francisco of today, a city like no other, is the story of The San Francisco Century.

BEAR PHOTO
S.F. 192

The old city was fair to see that last day of its life, Tuesday, April 17, 1906. It had been transformed in the previous ten years. The United States had annexed Hawaii and the Philippines, building an empire in the Pacific, and San Francisco saw itself as an imperial city. It had risen from the shantytown of the 1849 Gold Rush, had been made rich by the silver bonanza of Nevada's fantastic Comstock Lode, and was poised to become the New York of the Pacific Coast.

It had tall buildings: the elegant Ferry Building, where Market Street met the bay, only eight years old in '06 but already a symbol of the city; the famous Palace Hotel; the two-year-old St. Francis Hotel; and the striking Fairmont Hotel atop Nob Hill, scheduled to open later in the spring. The *Call* Building, at eighteen stories, was the tallest skyscraper west of Chicago; nearby were the brick *Chronicle* Building across Market Street, the new Flood Building down the block at Powell Street, and the huge Emporium department store on Market between Fourth and Fifth streets.

The imposing City Hall, which had taken twenty-seven years to build and cost a breathtaking

Opposite: Refugees huddle on Mint Street between Fifth and Sixth streets. The United States Mint, out of the picture on the left, was one of few major downtown buildings to remain intact. Top: Fires sweep into North Beach, seen from Russian Hill looking east, on the the first day. Telegraph Hill on the left horizon, and the Financial district, at right, are enveloped in smoke. Above: Enrico Caruso as Don Jose in *Carmen,* his last performance in San Francisco.

The temblor buckled streets and broke most of San Francisco's water mains, leaving fire brigades helpless. This view south on Van Ness Avenue near Broadway is one of the few photos depicting the city's dire water shortage. Opposite: A solitary pumper has a full head of steam, but the fire hoses are empty as flames lick at the top floors of the Fireman's Fund Insurance Company Building on California Street near Sansome Street.
At right: When the earth shuddered, falling masonry killed scores of people but also felled these unlucky cattle being driven to market along Mission Street in the pre-dawn hours of April 18. Pages 22-23: The Ferry Building stands in silhouette as the city is shrouded in smoke.

CATTLE KILLED ON MISSION ST. BY EARTHQUAKE

Stoddard

Copyrighted 1906
by
C.P. Magagno
Alameda

On Market Street, the rich and the poor flee toward the ferries that will take them to the safety of Oakland.
At right: Temperatures in excess of two thousand degrees Fahrenheit easily melted the girders in steel-framed buildings downtown.

$5.73 million — nearly $500 million in today's money — was the largest public building in the West. The Western Addition, beyond Van Ness Avenue, and the Mission district had blocks and blocks of new Victorian houses built of redwood from the forests of the North Coast. Outside "The City" (as it was known on the West Coast), new suburbs sprang up, such as Mill Valley and San Rafael, Alameda and the university town of Berkeley, all connected to the city by a combination of ferries and electric trains. Commuter trains down the Peninsula made it easy to live in the country and work in the city. "San Francisco," said the *Brooklyn Eagle*, "is the most cosmopolitan city in the country, outside of New York."

But it had a dark side as well.

Its fabled Chinatown, which tourists found "an exotic adventure full of the mystery of the unknown," was in reality an overcrowded slum, a dangerous place where thugs called "highbinders" acted as enforcers for competing criminal associations, according to John Kuo Wei Tchen, who wrote a

As the fires advanced, many residents hurriedly fled from their homes with the few possessions they could salvage. One woman, dressed in hat, coat, and cloak, sits dazed amid the ruins with all she had left: three trunks and a White treadle sewing machine. Nearby, other refugees are surrounded by their own possessions: a baby carriage, an umbrella, a pair of crutches.

A solitary figure surveys the ruins of Chinatown in this view by Arnold Genthe. The Hall of Justice, its dome tipped to one side, can be seen in the distance at center. The entire Chinese district was destroyed in the fire.

book on Chinatown. Opium was in wide use, and it was rumored that many young Chinese women were held as virtual sex slaves. Chinatown was a self-contained world, which was no surprise in view of the anti-Asian prejudice of many San Franciscans of the day. Chinese could not live outside Chinatown due to racial covenants in property deeds, and it was not wise for them to venture outside their district after dark. The Union Labor Party, which controlled city government, favored "the absolute exclusion of all Asiatics — Japanese as well as Chinese" from the United States.

The Sierra Club, with John Muir as president, extolled the beauty of nature from its office in San Francisco. At the same time, all the city's sewers flowed directly into the bay, a mixture of smoke and fog cloaked the city in winter, and the streets were coated with the droppings of thousands of dray horses that pulled the freight wagons and some streetcars. The city suffered an outbreak of bubonic plague in 1904, an event that went largely unreported in the press — such publicity was bad for business.

The Barbary Coast along Pacific Street, which gave the city an unparalleled reputation for colorful

At left: The grand new City Hall, built after decades of cost overruns, kickbacks, and shoddy construction, was reduced to a skeleton in seconds. The wreck of the City Hall was a symbol of a corrupt city run by political boss Abe Ruef and his handpicked cronies.

Top: Forlorn cable car No. 455 never made it out of the car barn that morning. This car and most of the city's cable car fleet were destroyed in the ensuing fire.

Above: Arnold Genthe's camera told the gruesome story of one of the many victims incinerated by the firestorm.

The cobblestone pavement is fractured along cable car tracks near Ninth and Brannan streets. The quake opened fissures in streets all over the city, and in many locations, the shifting earth twisted the rails.

wickedness, was in reality a civic disgrace, full of open prostitution and drug dealing. The town was wide open under the regime of Abraham Ruef, a famously crooked lawyer who controlled Mayor Eugene Schmitz and the Board of Supervisors. Ruef and his cronies took bribes from streetcar companies, from the gas and electric companies, from gambling dens and houses of prostitution, from corporations that did business with the city. The supervisors were so crooked that they took bribes from both sides in a telephone franchise case; it was bad form to take a bribe and then vote against the briber, and the losers complained.

Civic life in San Francisco was like grand opera, with heroes and villains and a gorgeous stage. So it was fitting that grand opera was on the program for April 17, the last evening of the city that was. It was the second night of the opera season, which had opened the night before with *The Queen of Sheba*, featuring a set that cost forty thousand dollars, ten thousand times the daily wage of a journeyman carpenter. The principal soloists were from New York's Metropolitan Opera. Alas, *Sheba* was panned by

At left: The top of Nob Hill, where the city's elite had dwelled, has become a refugee camp, as have many open areas. Tents have been pitched next to the gutted mansion of silver baron James C. Flood in what is now Huntington Park and, in the foreground, the present site of Grace Cathedral. The big building in the background is the uncompleted Fairmont Hotel. The interior burned, but the hotel was rebuilt and opened for business a year later.

Below left: Despite the stern demeanor of parental figures who must cook and sew under adverse conditions, the lounging children inside the tent suggest that many of the younger generation will remember the events of April 1906 as an extended camping trip.

Top right: Because damaged chimneys might cause more fires, cooking indoors was banned for several weeks. Enterprising San Franciscans coped with adversity by moving their stoves onto the sidewalk or, in this case, building a makeshift fireplace out of earthquake rubble next to now-useless cable car tracks. Below right: Restaurants, always an important feature of San Francisco life, rose from the ashes almost immediately. This sidewalk cafe's menu ranged from tamales for ten cents to ham and eggs for a quarter. Opposite: Meals for the homeless and destitute were dished out by the hundreds at outdoor dining facilities such as this one amid the hulking ruins of Union Square.

the San Francisco critics.

Tuesday's performance would be different. The opera was Bizet's *Carmen*, with the two-hundred-pound diva Olive Fremstad in the title role. The great Caruso, Enrico himself, was to sing Don Jose. Caruso was thirty-five and the highest-paid opera singer in the world. He spoke a colorful brand of English and delighted reporters by giving them cartoons he'd drawn. "To sing," he said, "it is good to sing. To draw the cartoons, that is difficult."

It was a beautiful night, warm and still, not a breath of wind. There was a crescent moon. The audience at the Grand Opera House on Mission Street near Third Street literally glittered, the women wearing diamond rings and chokers that caught the light when they moved and the men in white tie and tails. Caruso was magnificent. He got standing ovations, the audience cheering and shouting, "Bravo! Bravo!" He brought down the house.

"The audience forgot its diamonds ... it forgot everything but the electric performance of Caru-

At right: Emergency workers transport a quake victim via horse-drawn ambulance. Just after the earthquake, the big Mechanics' Pavilion, an auditorium at Grove and Larkin streets, was converted into a hospital. The building was near the ruined City Hall, just off Market. But when the fire moved closer, patients were moved to hospitals and hastily built facilities on the edge of the city. The one below was called "Camp Ingleside."

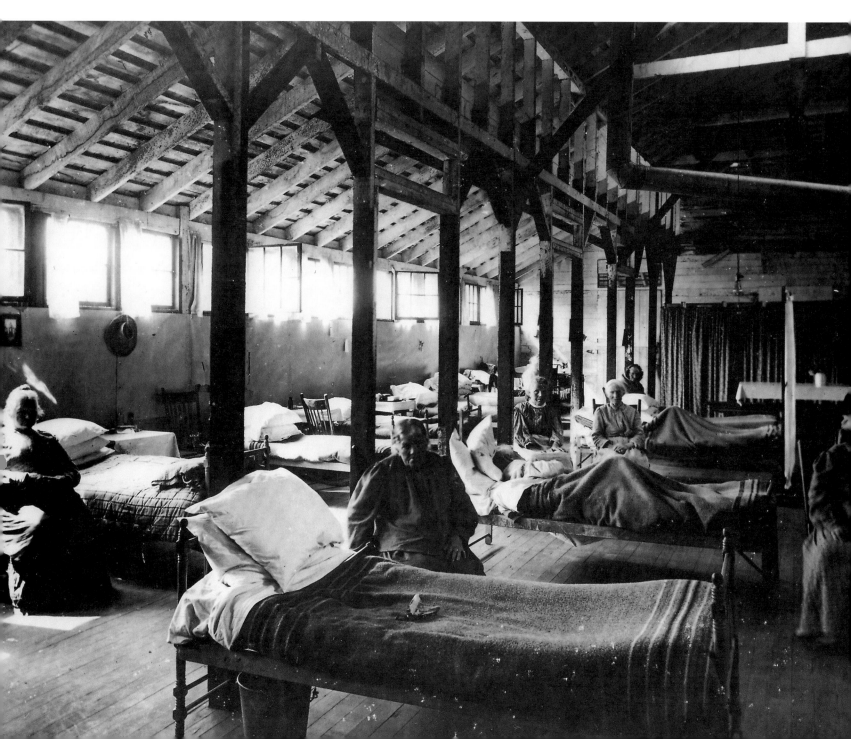

so, the wonderful," Blanche Partington wrote in the next day's issue of the *San Francisco Call*. The

Call, *The Chronicle*, and the *Examiner* were printed in the early morning hours of April 18, 1906, and

sent off by horse-drawn dray to subscribers in the city, by train down the Peninsula, by boat to the

East Bay and Marin.

Few would read them.

Just as the streetlights dimmed and the sky over the Oakland hills began to lighten, at 5:12:05 a.m.,

the San Andreas Fault slipped, and the earth shook. It sounded like thunder to police Officer Michael

Brady, like the roar of the sea to Officer Jessie Cook, "like a snarl" to *Call* reporter James Hopper. Race

Whitney and Wally Young, two other reporters who had just gotten off work, heard "a deep rumbling

in the distance," then "a concussive sound." Like a roll on the cymbals, *"mezzo forte,"* said Alfred Hertz,

who had conducted the opera orchestra the night before.

At Stanford University, down in Palo Alto, most of the new buildings collapsed in a heap of sand-

When the disaster wound down, residents were in desperate trouble — thousands of them had no homes and had to stand in line for the simplest necessities, including food. The people above are lined up on the 3600 block of Mission Street, near Thirtieth Street, in an area undamaged by the fires. Refugee camps were set up all over the city, in parks and open fields.

Almost as soon as the ashes cooled, adjusters from dozens of insurance companies set up tables in temporary facilities to assist their clients. The earthquake and fire amounted to the single largest insurance loss in American history up to that time. Only a few companies paid in full. According to historian Gladys Hansen, most of the ninety thousand claimants lost heavily. Some companies paid only ten cents on the dollar. Some paid nothing.

stone and a cloud of dust. To the north, the small town of Santa Rosa was knocked flat. And in San Francisco, the proud City Hall that had taken twenty-seven years to build fell down in seconds. Streets opened, power wires broke and snapped in the streets like electric snakes, brick walls fell, chimneys went down everywhere, church bells rang madly. Out on Pacific Avenue, Marion Leale, a young woman whose father was a ferry captain, looked out the window: "On the car tracks, a milk wagon stood drawn by two white horses, legs rigid, nostrils distended, fear personified."

"No terror equals that of an earthquake," Sydney Tyler wrote in *San Francisco's Great Disaster*.

In the Palace Hotel, Caruso was awakened in his suite by the sound and the motion. "I opened my eyes and said, 'What is it? What is it?'" He thought at first it was Martino, his valet, shaking him to wake him. "The next moment, I thought differently," he said later in an interview. "I sat up in the bed, which was rocking, like a ship at sea …" He went to the window. "My God! I thought it would never stop. I put my hand to my forehead — like that — and waited. It seemed like eternity … I ran to the

door and out into the corridor. Such screaming I never heard in my life before. Everywhere women, men, children, running about in their nightclothes … I snatched up my watch, my diamond pin, and my rings. Then I did what you call — skiddoo."

On Eleventh Street, the Reverend Charles N. Lathrop, rector of Advent Church, looked out his window in amazement: a roar, the crash of falling masonry, clouds of dust — he simply could not comprehend what had happened. "I thought I was crazy," he said.

What happened next was worse. Fires broke out all over the city. The quake had broken the water mains, and the city's fire department was helpless. The fire burned for three days and three nights and destroyed most of the city. When it was over, more than 250,000 people were homeless. The US Army said 498 people had died, although later estimates claimed the toll was more than three thousand.

It was the end of the old San Francisco and the beginning of an entirely new city.

Refugees found ways to amuse themselves, such as decorating their meager shelters. This palatial tent in Jefferson Square has been named "House of Mirth" and advises "Ring the Bell for Landlady," evidence that San Franciscans' sense of humor survived the disaster.

Above: The city in ruins is seen from a tethered balloon at fifteen hundred feet weeks after the fire: at left, ferries continue to run on the bay; at center, the burned-out shell of the new Fairmont Hotel rises atop Nob Hill; and in the distance at right stand the ruins of City Hall, which had been the largest public building in the West.

At right: Scaffolding wraps the Ferry Building as repairs commence on the tower's shattered facade. Nearby, soldiers (and their dog) are bivouacked along the Embarcadero.

N FRANCISCO
N FOREGROUND
E CAPTIVE AIRSHIP
ELEVATION
9, 1906.

In an eloquent expression of loss and comfort, photographer J.B. Monaco posed his son Dante and wife Katherine on a slope of Telegraph Hill, left. The diagonal street in the center is Columbus Avenue. Beyond is Russian Hill and beyond that the Golden Gate Strait and the Marin Headlands, still green in the spring weather.

PART TWO

Window on the Sea

The Embarcadero around 1906 had coastal steamers, deep-sea sailing ships, hay scows, and river barges tied up in the city's front yard. The vessels, from as far as the South Seas, were bound for ports from the North Coast to the sloughs of the Delta.

My father was a native San Franciscan and proud of it. "Anybody can be born in Oakland," he liked to say. The waterfront was his favorite place in the city. He even worked there, as a railroad switchman in the 1920s, a night watchman on ships in the '40s. His idea of fun was a Sunday walk on the Embarcadero. He could even recognize many of the old steam ferryboats by their whistles. "Do you hear that wheezy one?" he'd say. "That's the *Berkeley*, built in 1898, same year as me." He liked everything about the waterfront, even the ugly Embarcadero Freeway and the smells of the place — coffee roasting from the Hills Brothers plant, the salt water of the bay, the pungent creosote of the piers.

He's been gone for years, but if he came back, he'd recognize the new San Francisco. Market Street is still the main drag, the silvery Bay Bridge still goes to Oakland, and you can still take the Muni L car out to the zoo. But the waterfront would amaze him. The ships are gone, the Embarcadero Freeway is

A busy day on the southern Embarcadero in the 1930s. Big open trucks wait their turn to unload cargo on a pier. The cargo then was loaded aboard ships — a process that was expensive and time-consuming. The Embarcadero usually was jammed with truck and automobile traffic plus trains of the State Belt Railroad. Opposite: Twenty-one streetcar lines converged at the Ferry Building at the foot of Market Street in the 1920s, delivering their cargo of commuters to ferries headed for Oakland, Sausalito, Alameda, and Vallejo.

gone. The Ferry Building, a gray empty hulk when he was old, teems with people again. There are palm trees in the middle of the street and a baseball park down by the old banana-boat dock. The old waterfront greasy-spoon joints have been replaced by fancy restaurants that serve cuisine instead of hash.

In my father's day, San Francisco was the most important seaport on the Pacific Coast. The bay side of the waterfront looked like a saltwater forest, the masts of sailing ships standing like trees at nearly every pier. The waterfront, spared in the 1906 disaster, was lined with saloons, ship chandleries, and boardinghouses. Captain Fred Klebingat, who arrived in San Francisco aboard a four-masted sailing ship in 1909, told historian Karl Kortum: "If you walked into the Ensign saloon [at the foot of Market Street] and called 'Captain,' half the men in the place would look up." One could see long piers reaching out into the bay, workers loading cargo for countries around the world, steam trains shuffling freight cars all day and night, black smoke billowing from ships and ferryboats, trucks hauling cargo, and men going to work. Nearly fifty ferryboats crossed the bay daily. As late as 1930, San Francisco boasted that the Ferry

Building was the busiest terminal in the United States.

The waterfront was the city's window on the sea, a place that seemed to promise adventure. It was a working port, tougher than a ship owner's heart. Sailors and longshoremen frequently walked off the job — most memorably in the violent 1934 strike, marked by a riot on July 5 that included the "Battle of Rincon Hill." Police killed two men that day, which *The Chronicle* called "the darkest day this city has known since April 18, 1906," and which the unions came to call Bloody Thursday. The riot was followed by a three-day general strike that shut San Francisco down. The governor called out the National Guard. Revolution, some said, was in the air. For decades after that, waterfront workers, led by the fiery Australian Alfred Renton "Harry" Bridges, went on strike nearly every year. "It is a violent and incredible story, including the use of dynamite, tear gas, bullets, brickbats, strikebreakers, goon squads, the police, and the state militia," William Martin Camp wrote in *San Francisco: Port of Gold*. The waterfront — and its unions — went through booms and busts: good times right after the 1906 fire, when the city was be-

The waterfront unions gathered
strength in the spring of 1934
for an expected showdown
with the maritime industry.
Opposite: In May, thousands
of workers and their supporters
— including these two young
women — fill the Civic Center
area and march with flags
and high spirits.
At left: No one expected the
riots and bloodshed that would
follow in July, when authorities
attempted to open the port
after strikers shut it down.
In the "Battle of Rincon Hill,"
police (foreground) used tear gas
on the strikers, who then
retreated to the hilltop.
Above: Later, police opened fire
near the foot of Mission Street,
wounding two strikers, one
fatally. When the day's violence
was over, two men were dead,
and dozens were injured.
"Don't think of it as a riot,"
The Chronicle reported.
"It was a hundred riots."

The 1934 waterfront strike was led by Harry Bridges, who had come to San Francisco as a sailor in the '20s and by the mid-'30s was a powerful union leader. Bridges (meeting with strikers at Fort Mason in 1948, above) was hated and feared by the city's establishment. It was alleged that he had been a Communist and had lied on his citizenship papers. He was in court often and jailed briefly, but nothing ever was proved. Eventually, he became admired even by his enemies for his uncompromising honesty. When Bridges died in 1990, Mayor Art Agnos ordered city flags flown at half-staff. Opposite: The waterfront is bustling in 1948 — almost every pier has a ship tied up, waiting to be loaded or unloaded.

ing rebuilt, slow times in the early '20s and the '30s. The area was busier than ever during World War II, experienced a modest boom in the '40s, then suffered a long, slow decline, like a wasting disease. What finally killed the old waterfront was new technology. For more than one hundred years, a ship's cargo was carried in crates or sacks, loaded on pallets or slings, manhandled in and out of the cargo holds, then moved inside piers, which were like temporary warehouses. Each of a ship's five hatches employed a long-shore crew of up to twenty men. A ship would stay in port for a week, working cargo twenty-four hours a day. "Half the ship's operating time was devoted to being tied up at a pier," Fred Stindt wrote in *Matson's Century of Ships*. "There had to be a better way."

There was. Some East Coast lines had begun using containers — metal boxes that were loaded with cargo on shore, brought to the ships by rail or truck, and stowed on board by special cranes with minimal handling. A container ship could be loaded or unloaded in a day. The Matson Navigation Co. used containers for the first time in the Pacific on the freighter *Hawaiian Merchant*, which sailed from San

Francisco for Honolulu on Aug. 31, 1958. The ship was 491 feet long and carried a crew of fifty-one. Now container ships are double that length, and carry half the crew. They require special facilities — big gantry cranes, close rail connections — and San Francisco's port had been built to serve the past. Oakland built new facilities to attract the business, and the Matson line moved there in 1969. American President Lines, whose corporate parent had been a presence on the San Francisco waterfront since 1849, left the city for good, having been promised new facilities it never got.

The San Francisco waterfront deteriorated. The state built an elevated freeway along the Embarcadero in 1957, an eyesore that cut off the city from the bay. The last of the big, old, white ferryboats sailed for Oakland in 1958, and the Ferry Building, sliced up into offices, looked like a gray ghost of a building. The streets around the Ferry Building area turned dingy. The colorful Audiffred Building at Mission Street and the Embarcadero rented "studios" to poets, such as Lawrence Ferlinghetti. It also housed a shelter where drunks went to dry out. Artists moved into the empty old brick warehouses.

Opposite: Commercial fishing is one of the oldest and toughest jobs on any coast — skippers in small boats depend on skill, luck and good weather to make a living. This fisherman is icing down part of his catch of tuna in his boat's hold in 1950. Above: Longshoremen in 1934 rig gear to unload cargo, including food and stores for an oceangoing freighter as the ship's officer supervises the work.

An old-time San Francisco Bay automobile ferry steams up the north bay. Before the major bridges were built, as many as fifty ferryboats daily carried passengers, cars, and trucks across the water.

At right: A deckhand on the Southern Pacific Oakland ferry takes a look back at San Francisco on November 11, 1936, the day before the new Bay Bridge opened. It was twilight in more ways than one — the bridges eventually put the old ferry steamers out of business.

The Embarcadero Freeway,
connecting northern
San Francisco with the Bayshore
Freeway and Bay Bridge, cut off
the city from the bay. An ugly
landmark for more than three
decades, it was damaged in the
in 1989 Loma Prieta earthquake
and was torn down. Its demise
transformed the waterfront.

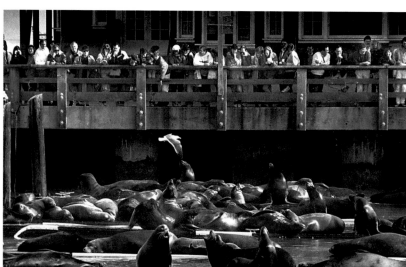

"There was the smell of dust, like living in your grandmother's attic," said Richard Perri, a painter who resided on the southern waterfront. The old waterfront became irrelevant to the new San Francisco. High-rise apartments were built along Clay and Washington streets where the old produce market used to be, and the next thing you knew, the residents were calling up to complain about the whistles of tugboats pulling out of Pier 9 on their early morning runs. "Complaining about boat whistles on the waterfront? I knew then that things had really changed," said Bill Figari, a retired ship captain who had spent his whole life on the bay. It took an act of God and only fifteen seconds to create the new Embarcadero: The 1989 Loma Prieta earthquake fatally damaged the Embarcadero Freeway. By 1992, it had been torn down, prompting *Chronicle* architecture critic Allan Temko to predict that "the central waterfront — and with it the whole heart of the city — will be open to a radiant future." That is exactly what happened: the Embarcadero was reborn, the roadway turned into a boulevard, complete with palm trees. The San Francisco Giants built a beautiful ballpark at China Basin, and the little cove at

Starting in the second half of the century, San Francisco became a major tourist destination and was advertised as "everybody's favorite city." On summer days, Fisherman's Wharf and its environs are crowded with visitors. Some of the favorite tourist sights: the sunbathing sea lions at Pier 39, opposite, below, and steaming live crabs at Fisherman's Wharf, above. In surveys, tourists say the Wharf is their favorite destination.

the mouth of Mission Creek, once an open sewer, was renamed for baseball hero Willie McCovey. On

game days, small pleasure boats jam the cove, hoping to catch a home run hit over the right-field wall.

Today, the waterfront begins at the San Francisco Maritime National Historical Park, which has

the largest collection of old ships in the world. It sweeps past Fisherman's Wharf and Pier 39, past the

Teatro ZinZanni, which advertises "Love Chaos & Dinner" nightly, past a pier where tugs berth, past

the revived Ferry Building, now crowded with patrons of its specialty stores, gourmet food shops, high-

end restaurants, and wine bar. It sweeps along a grand boulevard to its end at SBC Park. Just where the

silver Muni trains bound for the ballpark rise out of the dark subway into the sunlight at Folsom Street,

with the bay glistening and the great bridge sweeping overhead, a sculpture of a red-and-silver arrow in

a tan bow stands as tall as a building, the arrow piercing the earth. Streetcars, some old, some new, roll

up and down the northern waterfront, past the old piers, bringing people to the vibrant present in a

kaleidoscopic mixture, little bits of shifting light and color, images of different eras.

Opposite: Tourists meander from Pier 39 toward Fisherman's Wharf, the hottest tourist attraction in San Francisco. In 2004, more than fifteen million people visited the city, three-quarters of them patronizing the bars, restaurants, and shops of Fisherman's Wharf. Above: The bustling Ferry Building has become a paradise for gourmets and fresh-food lovers, including Lorian Newcomer, out for her weekly farmers' market shopping trip in 2004. Patrons also can imbibe at the wine bar or teahouse and dine in a choice of upscale restaurants. Pages 54-55: Seagulls hoping for a meal hover over the *High Flyer* as its crew repairs a fishing net in San Francisco Bay.

It's October 22, 2002, and the Giants are hosting the Anaheim Angels in Game Three of the World Series at Pac Bell Park. McCovey Cove, in the background, is filled with boats and hopeful fans wanting to retrieve a coveted home run ball from the bay. The fans were disappointed when the Giants lost this one 10-4 and came up short in the Series, four games to three.

At right: Seen from Sausalito across San Francisco Bay, sunrise on a brisk, clear January morning brings out a brave soul for a chilly swim.

Punctuating change on the waterfront is the sixty-foot-tall bow-and-arrow sculpture by Claes Oldenburg and Coosje van Bruggen. *Cupid's Span* was commissioned for the city by Donald and Doris Fisher, founders of The Gap, and installed in November 2002 in the pedestrian park on the Embarcadero, across from the end of Folsom Street. The artists told a *Chronicle* reporter that the bow is a stereotype of love, appropriate for a city often associated with the heart. They said its shape also evokes sailing ships and the Bay Bridge, which inspired them on an early visit to the site. They buried the point of the arrow and tip of the bow in the earth to play down any "aggressive content" and to "defunctionalize them." The dramatic fiberglass and stainless steel sculpture evokes both criticism and praise, including this from Mayor Gavin Newsom: "I love to hate that bow and arrow."

P A R T   T H R E E

City of Villages

Mission Street in the late 1920s was a rival to Market Street as one of the city's main thoroughfares. It was lined with stores and theaters and was the center of one of the city's small towns.

Beyond the famous views, the cable cars, and the other tourist attractions lies the real heart of San Francisco, a patchwork of neighborhoods, each with its own small main street, bus line, shops, restaurants, and bank branches. These neighborhoods are like self-contained small villages that together make up a seven-by-seven-mile city of more than seven-hundred thousand people. As the city has grown and changed over the past century, its neighborhoods have become more diverse and complex. One example of this evolution is Twenty-fourth Street in the southern part of the city. In just under two miles, this street runs through both the upscale Noe Valley and the largely Latino Mission district.

Twenty-fourth, lined by wooden buildings with a timeless look, is not a famous street. It's a shopping street of small stores and neighborhood restaurants downstairs with families living in flats upstairs. At the western end of the street is Twin Peaks, green in winter and spring, brown in the summer, when

the fog rolls over the hill, slowly, like a gray waterfall. Twin Peaks marks one end of Noe Valley, which

runs east to about Guerrero Street. East again, toward the bay, from Guerrero to the Bayshore Freeway,

Twenty-fourth is the heartland of the Latino Mission district.

Until the middle years of the San Francisco Century, Twenty-fourth was a blue-collar street, much

like every neighborhood south of Market. It was home to many of the people who worked in manufac-

turing, the shipyards and lumberyards, on the railroad and the waterfront. But then San Francisco

began to lose its industrial base, the port faded away, and the sons and daughters of working families

moved up into the middle class. The old Twenty-fourth Street split in two. The neighborhood between

about Guerrero Street and Potrero Hill, once largely Irish, became a Latino neighborhood, new people

living in old houses, the signs in Spanish. And Noe Valley changed as well. It used to be nothing special

by San Francisco standards, but today it is a gentrified neighborhood. The former drugstore at Twenty-

fourth and Castro streets is a dress shop, and what used to be hardware stores and shoe-

Noe Valley grew up after the 1906 earthquake and fire. It was a town inside a city, with its own neighborhood identity, including a Noe Valley baseball team, which competed with teams from other parts of the city. This squad was the pride of 1911.

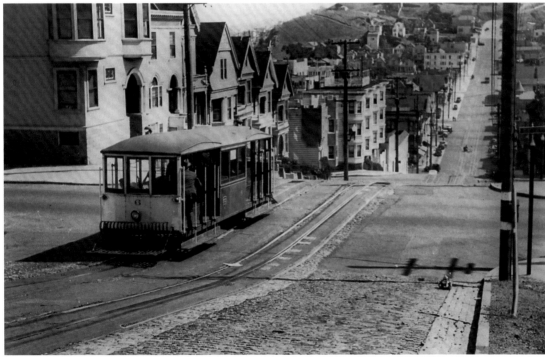

Except for the streetcar tracks and the boxy old cars parked at the curb, Twenty-fourth Street at Noe in 1929 looks much the same today.
At left: The Castro Street cable car climbs the hill to Twenty-third and Castro. The Castro cable ran from Twenty-sixth and Castro to Eighteenth Street until 1941, when buses powerful enough to climb the city's hills were developed.
Pages 62-63: Hand-lettered signs adorn Aleo's Market on Diamond Street in Noe Valley around 1939. The owners are John (third from left) and Lena (far right) Aleo.

Today, Twenty-Fourth Street in Noe Valley is an avenue of smart shops and boutiques, ideal for strolling and window-shopping even on a rainy day. At right: Fog drifts over Twin Peaks, partially obscuring the Sutro broadcast tower.

repair places now sell fancy cheese. In a couple of shops you can buy very nice wine, praised by critics for

its bouquet and perhaps a fleeting hint of strawberry.

At the beginning of 2005, the average single-family home in Noe Valley sold for $1.3 million, and

real estate agents said the prices were increasing 18 percent a year. These are old houses, some of them

new in the nineteenth century, where guys used to drink Dago Red, wine without a label, while in the

nearby saloons, men drank Old Crow, maybe, with a Burgie chaser. Paul Kantus, a tall, gray-haired re-

tired ship's engineer, now a neighborhood historian, can still recall the house his father built up on the hill

around the First World War for four thousand dollars. He remembers that some of the streets on

the fringes of the neighborhood were unpaved, and people kept chickens and goats. He is glad to show

newcomers his huge collection of photographs, which he calls the Noe Valley Archives. The old neigh-

borhood, he says, was like a village. "It still is a village," he said, "but a different one." When he was

young, he said, the neighbors were Irish and English, Italian and German, "all the mixture." His own

Jennifer Rivera manages the Rabat store at Twenty-fourth and Noe. Once a blue-collar neighborhood, Noe Valley has been transformed into an upper-middle-class district where houses sell for $1 million and up.

Top: Mission district boys, some wearing neckties and knickers, enjoy a sidewalk baseball game around the time of World War I. Above: In 1915, when the Mission was predominantly Irish American, a delivery truck advertises "Non-British tea."

name is Estonian. Today, Noe Valley's residents come mostly from other parts of the United States.

Noe Valley begins blending into other parts of the city at about Dolores Street, or maybe Guerrero, and then, heading east on Twenty-fourth, one enters the Mission district. For nearly eighty years, this was an Irish neighborhood with a bit of Italian thrown into the mix. Traffic flowed into Mission Street like a river, and the two halves of Twenty-fourth Street were tributaries. Mission was a big shopping street, called the Miracle Mile by merchants, lined with movie houses and stores, a rival to Market Street, a big important street like Fillmore Street on the other side of town. Few went to the other side of town then. Who needed it? Everything you wanted was on Twenty-fourth or, if not there, on the Mission Miracle Mile. "The Mission was my whole world," Frank Jordan said of his youth. He was the chief of police and then the mayor — the last, maybe, of the old-style San Francisco politicos. It was a complete world: people were born and raised in the Mission, baptized there, married there, raised a family there. There were Irish bars and Irish undertakers' parlors and the famous Irish wakes, where the

male mourners would skip the last part of the rosary at the funeral home, adjourn to a saloon, and toast the deceased. The Italians lived in the Mission, too, but they had their own ethnic neighborhood in North Beach — a place they called "the Little City," so the Mission considered itself green as the winter grass on the hills.

That whole world has vanished. Bearing witness to that is the Reverend Thomas Seagrave, born in the house his grandfather built in nearby Bernal Heights. He moved away, became a Catholic priest, and came back as pastor at St. Peter's, the Mission's Irish cathedral. He said he could date the change in the neighborhood to the mid-1950s, when Spanish surnames began appearing on the baptismal register at St. Peter's. It was not long before his whole congregation was Latino. Steve Canright, who grew up in the Mission, remembers the day a girl came into his first-grade class speaking only Spanish. It was 1953, and the other kids at Hawthorne School on Twenty-first Street were amazed. Meanwhile, the people who had been born and raised in the city — who even had their own

Most of the houses and flats in this picture of the inner Mission in the 1930s still stand. Until the 1940s, peddlers roamed San Francisco streets in horse-drawn carts. This one is selling Hawaiian bananas. The last horse carts were driven by junk men, whose cry of "rags, bottles, sacks!" still is remembered fondly by old-timers.

dialect, the Mission district accent — died or moved away. The old neighborhood seemed dangerous and shabby. Political unrest and poverty in Mexico and Central America brought new immigrants to San Francisco. They felt comfortable with the Spanish street names — Valencia, Guerrero, Potrero — left from the days when San Francisco was part of Spain and Mexico. The original settlers, whose ancestors had founded Mission Dolores in 1776, had been displaced by the newer Irish and Italians, who had come to the city because of poverty and political unrest in their own countries. So the cycle repeated itself.

The new Mission is on the walls of the old — hundreds of murals, perhaps as many as four hundred, in a riot of bright, defiant colors: tigers, eagles, Aztecs, local heroes, bare-breasted maidens, soldiers, and cops. "They reflect who we are and what we believe in," says Susan Chavez, who runs the Precita Eyes Mural Arts Center at Twenty-fourth and Harrison streets. It has been fifty years since the Latinos reclaimed the Mission, so a lot of native San Franciscans are bicultural, like Miguel Bustos, whose father was

Opposite: Teddi Bennett (left) and Tanja Nicklisch with their dog, Luna, dine outside the Truly Mediterranean restaurant on Sixteenth near Valencia in 1994. Above left: Dancers dressed as Aztec warriors perform in the annual Carnaval parade on Mission Street in 1998. Above right: A pedestrian saunters past a mural that brightens the neighborhood on Mission Street near Twenty-first.

Members of the group
Luz del Fuego help open
the Foreign Cinema restaurant
and outdoor movie theater
on Mission Street
in the summer of 1999.
Above, right: Bassist Mike
Jones entertains the crowd
at the Savanna Jazz club
on Mission Street
in the spring of 2004.

a farmworker from Mexico. Bustos is in his thirties and can remember an earlier Mission, after the Irish moved away but before the beginning of a creeping gentrification that now seems on the verge of changing the district again. People talk about buying a house in the Mission, a fixer-upper, a bargain for less than five hundred thousand dollars. But these people usually come from outside the neighborhood.

In 2005, one-third of the families in the Mission were making less than thirty-five thousand dollars a year. Two-thirds of the residents were renters. This is the main street of people who drive the city's trucks, wash the dishes in the city's restaurants, and work in the city's markets. Their chances of buying a home in the Mission have nearly vanished. "My grandchildren love the Mission," said Mission homeowner Jene Rita Alviar, who runs an after-school program on Twenty-fourth Street. "My daughter and son-in-law have good jobs, but they can't afford to buy a home in the Mission."

The Mission and Noe Valley: two towns on the same street, worlds apart.

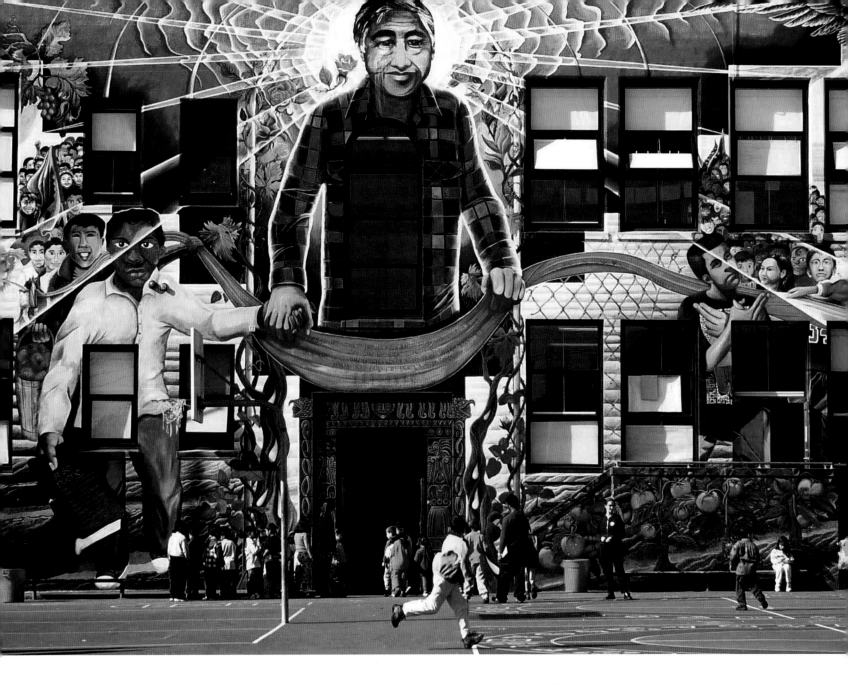

A mural of Cesar Chavez adorns the back of Cesar Chavez School in the inner Mission. At left: Alfredo Mendoza on bass, Andres Moreno (white hat) on the accordion, and Manuel Montes (black hat) on guitar form a band that plays in the bars and taquerias of the Mission nearly every night. They work for tips and ride Muni buses between gigs.

Monday morning in winter
in Bernal Heights, and the living
is good. Beagles Woody and
Darwin, awaiting their owner's
return, watch Carl Pickens
eat an outdoor breakfast
at the Moonlight Cafe
on Cortland Avenue.
At right: Maria Mango, a
23-year-old street musician,
sings on Haight Street
in the Haight-Ashbury in 2004.
Pages 74-75: Ryan Meshband,
who came from Australia
to celebrate Halloween
in the Castro district, sports
a cowboy hat and joins revelers
in the middle of Castro Street.

Forty-eight Towns in Search of a City

The Chamber of Commerce calls the neighborhood pattern in the city "a mosaic." The chamber counts forty-eight separate neighborhoods, from Alamo Square to Yerba Buena. Here is a sampling:

Bernal Heights grew up after the 1906 fire and had its own gold rush in the nineteenth century. Once noted for its grazing cows and goats, it has sweeping views and high real estate prices.

Bayview-Hunters Point once was the location of all the city's slaughterhouses — Butchertown was a neighborhood inside a neighborhood — and an opera house that still stands on outer Third Street. After World War II, this district became the center of African American San Francisco.

The Castro was a working-class neighborhood that became a mecca for gays beginning in the '60s. One of the city's most vibrant and colorful districts, its center is Eighteenth and Castro streets.

The Excelsior is in the outer Mission, largely a blue-collar district.

Glen Park, in a little valley south of South of Market, calls its main shopping district a village.

Chinatown for a century was the largest Chinese district outside of Asia. Through the changes in

Colorful Victorian houses decorate Alamo Square along Steiner Street as the city's skyline provides a modern backdrop.

Brent Byars prepares
an order in a timeless scene
in the Molinari Delicatessen
on Columbus Avenue
in North Beach. The famous
deli celebrated its centennial
in 1996.

San Francisco over the last one hundred years, Chinatown has retained its distinct look and feel.

The Fillmore and **the Western Addition**: For some time in the nineteenth century, Van Ness Avenue was the western edge of the city, but in the 1870s, developers began to sell lots in a new area — the Western Addition. It runs from Van Ness west to about Presidio Avenue, south to roughly the edge of the Golden Gate Panhandle, north to ritzy Pacific Heights. During World War II, African Americans moved in, and Fillmore became the big street of a mini-Harlem, with clubs, bars, and a lively street life.

The Haight was a middle-class district until the late 1960s, then became the epicenter of the Summer of Love, and the intersection of Haight and Ashbury streets became a world-famous destination for flower children. The district is divided into two areas — the upper and lower Haight.

Ingleside, in the southwestern part of the city, was undeveloped until after the 1906 fire. It's near the ocean and San Francisco State University.

The Marina did not exist until it was developed for the 1915 Panama-Pacific International Exposi-

A child races alongside the antique carousel at the San Francisco Zoo in 1975. Below: Sunbathers bask in Mission Dolores Park, near where the fire was halted in 1906, as downtown buildings stand out against the blue sky of a late summer in 2000.

Signs of spring: Annette Smith
waters vegetables in the median
strip of Quesada Avenue
in the Bayview; at right,
the cross on Mount Davidson,
the highest point in the city, is
illuminated in the fog for sunrise
services on Easter 1975.

tion from landfill. It had an Italian flavor for years (Joe DiMaggio had a home there), but after the 1989 earthquake, many of the old families moved away and were replaced by younger single people.

Mission Bay began as a shallow inlet, became a railroad yard, and now, with a campus of the University of California, is the city's newest neighborhood.

Nob Hill, with cable cars, big hotels, famous views, and spiffy apartments, is the quintessential San Francisco neighborhood, followed closely by **Telegraph Hill**, **Russian Hill**, and **North Beach**. A century ago, the rich lived on Nob Hill, the poets and philosophers on Russian Hill, and the struggling bohemians on Telegraph Hill. Only the rich can afford those places now.

North Beach has changed radically. Once a self-contained "Little Italy" with two daily Italian-language newspapers, it still has Italian restaurants and street signs, but now many of its residents are Chinese. Around Washington Square, its heart, you can see everything from cable cars to breathtaking views to elderly women performing slow and graceful T'ai Chi movements.

San Francisco is famous for its cuisine, a place where chefs are celebrities. First, however, they must learn the trade. Here Ashely Lyon (front) and three other apprentice chefs take a break in front of the California Culinary Academy on Polk Street in the Civic Center area.

San Francisco may be in the West, but the range here is all pavement. Seven-year-old Aliza Lauter (at right) enjoys a ride on a mechanical horse in a coffeehouse on Clement Street in 2005. Below: "At the end of our streets are spars," poet George Sterling wrote about the city and its rows of sailing ships of a century ago. At the end of the streets on Potrero Hill are high-rise buildings.

Potrero Hill has knockout views and knockout housing prices. It was home to billy goats and Russian émigrés in the '20s and '30s, and around World War II, public housing projects were built on the top of the hill. O.J. Simpson was raised there.

The Richmond, on the north side of Golden Gate Park, looks a bit like a strip mall in places. Its main shopping streets, Clement Street and Geary Boulevard, have an Asian feel to them, though the district also has a thriving Irish pub scene.

The Sunset, on the south side of the park, was bleak and barren before 1906, and until the '40s much of it was sand dunes. The **Inner Sunset**, nearest to downtown, is noted for neighborhood restaurants — one block of Ninth Avenue contains more than a dozen. The **Outer Sunset**, considered at one time to be a suburb in the city, consists mostly of tract homes built in the late '30s and '40s. At the end of its streets is the Pacific Ocean, and on clear days, you can spot the Farallon Islands. Don't count on clear days, though. The Richmond and Sunset are the foggiest areas in town, especially in the gray San Francisco summer.

Fawn Pierre and the dogs she is training — Kiko, Pico, and Leo — enjoy a breezy walk along Crissy Field just inside the Golden Gate in October 2003.
Pages 82-83: A dramatic view of San Francisco shows the Palace of Fine Arts in the foreground, looking east toward the Bay Bridge. The edge of the Presidio is to the lower right.

PART FOUR

City of Cultures

I n San Francisco, nothing is exactly as it seems. According to sani-
tized versions of the city's history, San Francisco always has celebrated its Asian populace, especially Chinatown, with its other-

**Grant Avenue, the main street of
San Francisco's Chinatown, on a
quiet afternoon in the 1930s.
Older Chinese Americans knew
the street as *Dupon Gai*, or
Dupont Street, its original name.**

worldly back alleys, colorful shopping streets, and flavor of another culture. The truth is more complex.

Herb Caen wrote in his best-selling book, *Baghdad by the Bay*: "Chinatown. Beloved indulgently and

condescendingly by the rest of San Francisco — as long as its inhabitants stay in their own places and

make no attempt to cross the invisible boundaries into the 'white' city." Caen wrote that in 1949, but

many native San Franciscans who grew up in Chinatown will tell you that until about the '60s, it was

unwise for a Chinese kid to cross Broadway into North Beach and next to impossible for a Chinese fam-

ily to live west of Van Ness Avenue. If that kid crossed the invisible line that marked his neighborhood,

he was liable to be beaten up by white kids. Chinese families trying to move into white San Francisco

discovered that real estate agents would not show them houses. It was as if a wall surrounded China-

BULLETINS ABOUT THE HOMELAND
SAN FRANCISCO CHINATOWN

People stop to read the news about China and the world posted in the window of the *Chinese World* newspaper in this postcard scene of Chinatown sometime after 1910.

town, part custom, part racism. Now San Franciscans love to tell visitors how the chief of police is a Chinese American woman who went to a Catholic school. They forget that until 1957, a century after the San Francisco Police Department was formed, the city didn't have a single Chinese American officer, and members of the SFPD's Chinatown Squad — all white men — hung out on street corners watching for Chinese gambling and other crimes. Asians effectively were barred from the police department by height limitations — a candidate had to be at least five feet nine inches tall. This policy was set aside by a series of federal court rulings in the 1970s.

Chinese have the deepest roots of any immigrants in the West: a few lived in California even before the 1849 Gold Rush. The city's Chinese always reminded others that Asia was just beyond the Golden Gate. And San Francisco's Chinatown was where the two worlds met. For 150 years, it has been the economic and cultural heart of the Chinese world in California: a lively music and arts scene, a district of good restaurants and places to do business, the center of social life. Chinatown was in the heart

During the years when Chinese immigration was severely limited, Chinese America was mostly a bachelor society with very few children. This group wears traditional clothes favored by Chinese Americans just after the opening of the twentieth century. Note the contrast to the men on the opposite page. At left: Employees pose in the Sam Hop Co. store on Clay Street in 1908. Pages 88-89: A young woman buys vegetables at an outdoor stand in the self-contained world of Chinatown.

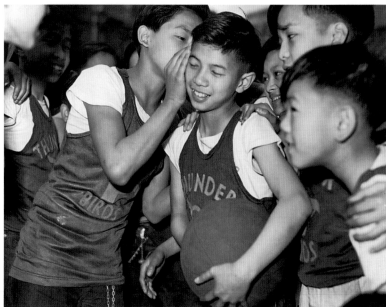

of San Francisco, and Dong Kingman, the artist, "loved the mist-shrouded hills and vistas of San Francisco because they reminded him of Chinese landscapes," according to his son, Dong Kingman Jr.

It was as colorful as a postcard, but it had a bitter edge. "San Francisco wasn't always so liberal," said Him Mark Lai, a native San Franciscan and a Chinese American scholar and historian. It is difficult now to imagine the anti-Asian attitudes at the dawn of the twentieth century. Anti-Chinese riots broke out in nearly every California city and town in the late nineteenth century. In Seattle, the municipal government forcibly expelled the Chinese from the city. In San Francisco in the 1870s, an agitator named Dennis Kearney led mobs armed with pickaxes in marches on Chinatown. Asians were not permitted to attend San Francisco public schools until the federal government intervened in 1906 after protests from Japan's government. They couldn't belong to most labor unions until World War II. In 1902, Samuel Gompers, president of the American Federation of Labor, told a U.S. Senate committee that "the Chinese are a monstrous evil ... utterly

Opposite: A festival — the Chinese Rice Bowl Party — lights up Grant Avenue in May 1942.
At left: A Chinese parade winds along Van Ness Avenue in 1912.
Below: Bertha Lew (left) and Laura Wong show off traditional and more modern styles of dress in the period just after the 1911 Chinese revolution.
Pages 94-95: Another generation — Chinese American boys and girls dress up for a revue that appears to have included Uncle Sam.

incapable of adaption to the Caucasian's ideas of civilization."

Starting in 1882, and until the Chinese Exclusion Act was repealed in 1943, most Chinese were barred from immigrating to the United States and could not become naturalized citizens. Exceptions included merchants, their family members, and children of native-born citizens. The 1906 earthquake and fire proved to be an unexpected boon to Chinese Americans as well as Chinese who wanted to immigrate: not only did the fire destroy the shabby old Chinatown, but the city's records — of births, deaths, marriages — burned. Thus a resourceful prospective immigrant could pay an American-born Chinese to claim he was a member of the family, and no records existed to disprove that claim. The immigrant then took the new family name and became what was called a "paper son." Many Chinese Americans will tell you that thousands of people came to this country with false identities. "The Chinese I knew hid their names," Maxine Hong Kingston wrote in *The Woman Warrior*. "Sojourners take new names whenever their lives change and guard their real names with silence."

San Francisco's Chinese have always shared their festivals with the world. Students at Clarendon Alternative Elementary School show off a baby dragon of their own creation in 1988.

The wide use of false names contributed to making the insular world of Chinatown even more isolated from the city outside; it was not a good idea to draw attention to oneself. "You had to be very careful," the historian Lai remembered. Even members of the second generation, born in California, had an innate caution about who they were. "You did not want to bring problems on your family." His own father was a paper son. His real family name is Mark, pronounced "Mok." Early in the century, nearly all all of the Chinese in the western United States came from four provinces — the so-called Sze Yup region — near Canton, now called Guangzhou, in southern China. They had strong regional and family ties, and a San Francisco-based group of family associations, the Six Companies, functioned as a council of elders for the community. In the outside world, the city fathers — and all of them were men — went to these elders when they wanted to get something done in Chinatown.

When the Japanese attacked Pearl Harbor in 1941, prejudice against Asians flared up again. Japanese on the West Coast, citizens and noncitizens alike, were shipped off to detention camps. Though

other Asians were not affected, they looked upon the Japanese American experience as a cautionary

tale. But the climate was changing gradually. In 1957, Herb Lee, born and raised in Chinatown, became

the first Asian American police officer in San Francisco. Lee, now retired, still remembers that on his

first day on the job, a veteran cop yelled out, "Where is that Chinaman?" But he is proud of his role as

a police officer and as a pioneer and mentor to new Asian American officers. "Now there are hundreds

of Chinese and Japanese and Filipino officers in San Francisco," he said. "And two, Fred Lau and

Heather Fong, rose to the pinnacle of the department as police chief."

In the mid-1960s, the mix of the Asian population began to change. Chinese immigration had been

restricted even after the repeal of the Exclusion Act — the entire quota for Chinese immigrants to the

United States was 105 people a year. In 1965, that quota was lifted, resulting in a huge influx of Asian

immigrants. On the eve of World War II, Lai points out in his book, *Becoming Chinese American*, only

106,334 Chinese lived in the United States. By the opening of the twenty-first century, there were

**At top: A young man spins
and whirls a string of exploding
red firecrackers at a Chinese
New Year's celebration
at Portsmouth Square in 1991.
Above: Susan Yao
of the St. Mary's Drill Team
finds something about the
2004 New Year's parade
too funny for words.**

New waves of Asian immigration have meant the growth of Chinese districts outside Chinatown, such as Clement Street in the Richmond district, home to the New Sunny Land & Co. market.
Below: A boy and his grandfather share a quiet moment at North Ping Yuen courtyard in Chinatown in 1997.
Opposite: Grant Avenue is decorated for the Moon Festival in the fall of 2003.

2.5 million. In San Francisco, the Asian population of the city — 4.8 percent in 1950 — reached 30.84 percent, or 239,565, in 2000, two-thirds of them Chinese. This is enough to support six local daily Chinese-language newspapers — some pro-Taiwan, some pro-mainland, others reflecting various political groups.

As more Asians entered the middle class, the older generation began to abandon Chinatown. New Chinese neighborhoods sprang up across the city, particularly in the Richmond and Sunset districts. Whole shopping streets and main drags of San Francisco neighborhoods, such as Clement Street in the Richmond, became predominantly Chinese. Native San Francisco Chinese Americans, Lai says, sometimes find Chinatown, once again a largely immigrant community, almost foreign. The future, Lai thinks, will be different still. "You start to be different from the people in China the first day you are here. From the first day, you are a different person."

For San Francisco's Chinese, once excluded from the rest of the city and its power structure, life has

changed dramatically: when Gavin Newsom was elected mayor in December 2003, he made sure one of his first public appearances as mayor-elect was a walk through Chinatown to thank his supporters there. "There is going to be a change in the culture of city government," he said.

The Many Faces of San Francisco

San Francisco always has been ethnically diverse. The city's population at the time of the 1906 earthquake was nearly 95 percent white, but it was representative of the many nations of Europe. The old German Hospital, which became the Davies Medical Center and then part of the California Pacific Medical Center, displayed a picture of the Kaiser in the front lobby. The city had a large French community, also with its own hospital and a daily French-language newspaper. Two Italian-language daily newspapers were published in San Francisco, and in North Beach, a foreigner was someone who spoke only English. A large Irish population filled the Mission district, and the Irish had their own

Opposite, above: Portsmouth Square is the original center of San Francisco, where the American flag was first raised in the city, where Robert Louis Stevenson spent idle time, and where the world's first cable car line began. For years, it has been the heart of Chinatown; here old men talk and take in the sun in the summer of 1976. Opposite, below: A lion dancer gyrates in the Double Ten Parade in Chinatown on October 10, 1976. Above: At the beginning of the San Francisco Century, mayors denounced the city's Chinese. In 2003, Mayor-elect Gavin Newsom walks along Stockton Street to thank Chinese Americans for their support.

San Francisco is like a
tapestry: many colors,
many ethnic groups.
Above: Amanda Yasutake
prepares to lead her troupe
from the Hanayagi Dance Studio
at the Cherry Blossom Festival
in Japantown in spring 1994.
At right: Third-graders
Wayne Hodges and
David Coomber
from William R. DeAvila
Elementary School marvel
at herons in a treetop nest
near Stow Lake
in Golden Gate Park.

newspaper. So many Swedes, Danes, and Norwegians sailed out of San Francisco that the small coastal

schooners based in the city were called "the Scandinavian Navy." It was "the hugest smelting-pot of

races," wrote Robert Louis Stevenson, who lived in San Francisco in the nineteenth century.

The ethnic mix in the city seems to run in cycles, like the tides. San Francisco was a homogenous

place in the 1920s and 1930s, the heyday of native-born generations. Then came World War II, which

brought thousands of new people to the region. Most prominent among them were African Americans,

who moved out of the South in what scholars call the Great Migration. As late as 1930, fewer than

1 percent of San Franciscans were black. By 1970, black people were more than 13 percent of the pop-

ulation and were the city's largest single minority.

Today there is a new San Francisco. You can see it clearly on the Muni Metro subway, on the streets,

in the big department stores, nearly anywhere in the city. The numbers tell the story: in the 2000 US

Census, the majority of San Franciscans were non-white. The city was still diverse, but in a different way.

Top: Participants enjoy
2004's Cherry Blossom Parade,
a springtime tradition
in Japantown.
Above: Brendan Cunningham,
five years old, pilots his toy
police car in the St. Patrick's
Day Parade in 2005.

With its golden onion domes, the Russian Orthodox Cathedral of the Holy Virgin on Geary Boulevard presents a striking contrast to the rows of apartment houses in the Richmond district. Opposite: Alexa Drapiza gives three-year-old Daniel Cruz a hug at a Flores de Mayo celebration at Bessie Carmichael School in the South of Market district. Flores de Mayo is a traditional spring event in the Filipino community.

Nearly one in three San Franciscans was of Asian descent, 14 percent were Latino, and not quite half were of European descent. Nearly half the population of San Francisco spoke a language other than English at home, and 36.8 percent of the city's residents were foreign-born. Meanwhile, not only has the white population declined, but so has the number of African Americans. The black population, which peaked at 96,078 in 1970, dropped thirty years later to less than 8 percent, squeezed out by employment changes and the high cost of housing. Vietnamese, on the other hand, numbered nearly eleven thousand in the last census, twice as many as in 1990. A Little Saigon sprang up near City Hall and in the Tenderloin. Though people from the Philippines make up the fastest-growing Asian population in California, most of the growth of the Filipino population has been in other Bay Area communities. San Francisco's Filipino population, about forty thousand, was the same size in 2005 as it was a generation ago. Other ethnic groups have declined in size — the Japanese American population, once centered around Nihonmachi in the Western Addition, dropped 5 percent between 1980 and 2000.

SAN FRANCISCO'S POPULATION BY RACE

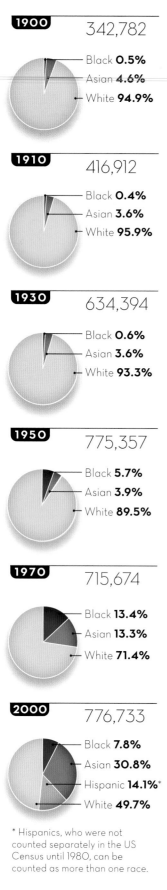

1900 — 342,782

- Black **0.5%**
- Asian **4.6%**
- White **94.9%**

1910 — 416,912

- Black **0.4%**
- Asian **3.6%**
- White **95.9%**

1930 — 634,394

- Black **0.6%**
- Asian **3.6%**
- White **93.3%**

1950 — 775,357

- Black **5.7%**
- Asian **3.9%**
- White **89.5%**

1970 — 715,674

- Black **13.4%**
- Asian **13.3%**
- White **71.4%**

2000 — 776,733

- Black **7.8%**
- Asian **30.8%**
- Hispanic **14.1%** *
- White **49.7%**

* Hispanics, who were not counted separately in the US Census until 1980, can be counted as more than one race.

But counting people is notoriously difficult. For example, Arabs are not commonly identified with San Francisco, and Arab American leaders say they have been undercounted in the census. The Arab Cultural and Community Center in San Francisco believes there are 120,000 people of Arabic descent in the Bay Area. "It's a very vibrant community," said Abeer Rafidi, the center's director. "Over five hundred restaurants and corner markets are Arab-owned in just the city."

These businesses, mostly corner stores and small restaurants, are traditional in San Francisco. They look much the same as they did decades ago, when they were run by Irish, Italian, and Chinese proprietors. They are still run by immigrant families — it's only the people in charge who have changed.

Slices of life in two San Francisco institutions: Eight-year-old Tyler Reynolds (opposite) peels an egg while waiting for the Easter service to begin at Glide Memorial United Methodist Church in April 2003, and Giovanni Giotta (above), the owner of Caffe Trieste, sings for customers in the North Beach landmark in 2004.

The Chitresh Das Dance
Company practices traditional
Indian dance at the Cultural
Integration Fellowship
near Golden Gate Park in 2005.
At right: On another day,
outdoors and in the park,
Saeed Bus and his three-year-old
son, Zubar, share a meal
at a celebration of Pakistani
Independence Day
in the summer of 2002.

At left: Mounia Elnatour shows off her new hijab after Friday prayers at the San Francisco Islamic Society on Jones Street in the Tenderloin in 2004.
Top: Jackson Milford (left), office manager of the Vietnamese Elderly Mutual Assistance Association, receives food from a Project Open Hand volunteer in San Francisco's Little Saigon in 2004.
Above: Andres Sanchez-Paiva lights a candle inside Mission Dolores basilica as his little brother, Simon, observes in 2005.

PART FIVE

The Power and the Glory

I n the spring of 1906, San Francisco was a mess. The city was in ruins, its records had burned in the fire that followed the earthquake, the new City Hall had collapsed, and city government was in the hands of corrupt politicians. Mayor Eugene Schmitz was removed from office in 1907, tried and convicted on corruption charges; he got a new trial on a technicality and was acquitted. Only political boss Abe Ruef went to prison. Three mayors served during the next five years — one, ex-Supervisor Charles Boxton, quit after only a week.

The Bay Bridge opens November 12, 1936, symbol of a growing and ambitious city. For the first time, people could drive between San Francisco and the East Bay.

In 1912 came James Rolph Jr., the most colorful mayor in the city's history. A millionaire when he took office, Rolph had a small white mustache and loved to wear cowboy boots and a carnation in his lapel. "Sunny Jim," as they called him, had charm to spare. He also got things done. San Francisco opened the new Civic Center, hosted the 1915 Panama-Pacific International Exposition, and secured San Francisco's water supply with the Hetch Hetchy project. Rolph and the city engineer,

The Hetch Hetchy Valley in Yosemite National Park, considered by John Muir one of nature's cathedrals, was dammed by the city of San Francisco for a reservoir in 1923. Above is the Hetch Hetchy Valley in its original state; at right is how it appeared later. After the dam was built, it took nearly twenty years to complete the project to bring water and power to the Bay Area. The driving force behind the massive undertaking was San Francisco Mayor James Rolph Jr., shown opposite early in his reign at City Hall. Rolph had a wonderful time being mayor. He loved fast cars, a good drink (even during Prohibition), and playing host to mayors, kings, and movie stars.

an imperious Irishman named M.M. O'Shaughnessy, put their mark on San Francisco — new streets, new police stations, new firehouses. O'Shaughnessy's engineering staff designed the Twin Peaks and Sunset railway tunnels and opened up the Sunset district, which had been a wilderness of sand dunes, to development. Rolph made sure people knew who deserved the credit: he donned a Muni cap and drove some of the first streetcars through the tunnels himself. Rolph even had his own theme song, "Smiles" — "There are smiles that make you happy," it begins. He was re-elected by a bigger margin every campaign, running the city for a record nineteen years.

Sunny Jim capped his career in 1930 when he was elected governor of California. But he was a failure in that job. He couldn't deal with the state Legislature or the Great Depression. His health broken, he died in 1934, and his body lay in state in the rotunda of his monument — San Francisco City Hall. In his will, he wrote "Good-bye, good luck, God bless you all." At his death, he owed his barber $50 and his bootblack $138.60 for keeping his cowboy boots shiny.

1915 — When the World Came to San Francisco

Less than nine years after it was all but destroyed, San Francisco built a dream city on its northern shore, six hundred acres of domes and pastel buildings that stretched from Van Ness Avenue to the Presidio, from Chestnut Street to the bay. The centerpiece was the fantastic forty-three-story Tower of Jewels. The most lovely building was Bernard Maybeck's stunning Palace of Fine Arts, designed to look like elegant ruins, a piece of instant nostalgia made of cement and chicken wire.

This was the Panama-Pacific International Exposition of 1915, "a temporary Byzantium ... a vision of what

San Francisco wanted to be, but couldn't be," said Gray Brechin, who wrote a history of the city called *Imperial San Francisco*. Among the attractions were sculpture by Rodin, John Philip Sousa leading his band, a Ford assembly line that produced a new car every ten minutes, airplanes, a miniature of the Panama Canal, the first transcontinental telephone call, and *Stella,* a painting of a nude woman so lifelike that she appeared to breathe.

The fair, which ran for ten months, made so much money that its directors presented San Francisco with a grand auditorium in the Civic Center that still

stands, now named in honor of local rock music impresario Bill Graham. On the last night, the colored lights were turned off one by one as half a million people — more than the population of San Francisco — watched the twinkling city fade to black. "Plaster dreams, soon to be dust," wrote Robert Duffus in *The Tower of Jewels,* his book about the city of those days. The Palace of Fine Arts was too beautiful to destroy, and it stands, even now, by its lagoon in the Marina. The elephant sculptures that guarded one of the fair's buildings now guard a little park near the ferry landing in Sausalito.

Opposite: The 1915 Panama-Pacific International Exposition's lasting memorial is Bernard Maybeck's Palace of Fine Arts in the Marina district. The centerpiece of the fair, however, was the Tower of Jewels, at left, adorned with 102,000 gemlike pieces of glass that amazed fairgoers with a show of sparkling light. This image is from a linen postcard mailed from San Francisco in 1915. Below: One of the wonders of the fair was daredevil flier Lincoln Beachey, who performed stunts nearly every day, once flying his plane inside a building. Beachey's run ended tragically when he put his aircraft into a "death dive." It crashed into the bay, and Beachey was killed.

Governor Frank Merriam uses a blowtorch to cut a chain and open the Bay Bridge on November 12, 1936. Flanking him are (from left) Mayor Angelo Rossi of San Francisco, chief bridge engineer Charles Purcell, former President Herbert Hoover, Oakland Mayor William MacCracken, Charles Henderson, director of the U.S. Reconstruction Finance Commission, U.S. Senator William Gibbs McAdoo, and state public works director Earl Lee Kelly. At right: Mayor Roger Lapham (seated, at left) poses in 1947 for Naval Reserve Week with (from left) Dan London of the St. Francis Hotel, comedian Red Skelton, Navy Rear Admiral Donald Beary, and Harold Russell, star of the movie *The Best Years of Our Lives.*

Other mayors who made a difference:

ANGELO J. ROSSI: Rolph's handpicked successor, he was mayor in the worst of times and the best

of times. He saw the depths of the Depression and the bloody waterfront strike of 1934. But he also presided

over the opening of the great bridges that defined San Francisco — the Bay Bridge, in the fall of 1936,

and the Golden Gate, just seven months later. In 1939-40, a world's fair sparkled on Treasure Island. Rossi,

mayor for thirteen years, hung on for one election too many and was turned out of office in 1944.

ROGER D. LAPHAM: A silver-haired, distinguished-looking businessman who vowed to serve

only one term, he was host of the conference that formed the United Nations in 1945. Lapham ran

the city like a business but made one terrible mistake: he announced in 1947 that the cable cars

were dangerous and obsolete and pushed to have them abolished. "You can't do that to San Fran-

cisco," said Friedel Klussmann, a women's club member who lived on Telegraph Hill and who led

others in opposition. She was right, Lapham was wrong, and he never lived it down. He was suc-

"The Main Street of the Bay Area"

People talk about the Golden Gate Bridge as a symbol of the Bay Area, but to E.R. "Mike" Foley, who for years was chief engineer of all the state bridges, the Bay Bridge is the remarkable one. "The Golden Gate has a marvelous location, but the Bay Bridge is a far more wonderful engineering achievement," Foley said.

When it opened in 1936 at a cost of $78 million and the lives of twenty-four workers, the Bay Bridge was the largest bridge ever built, a monument to engineering and to the spirit of difficult times — the depths of the Depression. "People then had guts and foresight," Foley said on the Bay Bridge's sixtieth

birthday in 1996. "The Bay Bridge alone was one of the largest public works projects in the world, but to build them both at the same time ... now you can't get them to build anything." The Bay Bridge is several bridges in one: the western half between San Francisco and Yerba Buena Island really is two suspension bridges that meet in a concrete island in the middle of the bay. It was designed with four towers and four spans between them. The tunnel through the island was the largest — though not the longest — in the world. It connects the western half with the eastern cantilever bridge, which in turn connects with five smaller truss spans leading to the Oakland

shore. One of these truss spans failed in the Loma Prieta earthquake in 1989, leading to plans for a retrofit of the whole bridge.

Whatever the future holds, the Bay Bridge, which carries 275,000 vehicles a day and is the busiest toll bridge in the world, will remain the most important bridge in the region. "The main street of the Bay Area," the late engineer Robert Halligan called it. "The grandmother of all the bridges on the bay." Halligan and Foley had the idea of stringing lights on the bridge like a necklace spanning the bay for bridge's fiftieth birthday in 1986. The lights were so beautiful that half a million dollars was raised to make them permanent.

Opposite: As ferries steam between its towers, the bridge begins to rise over the bay in 1934. It actually will be several bridges when completed — this part from San Francisco to Yerba Buena Island consists of two suspension bridges connected to a concrete central anchorage. Cables already have been strung to the Alpha and Bravo towers on the San Francisco side.

At left: Sixty-four years after the Bay Bridge opened, veteran painter Karen Juzefczyk (foreground) and apprentice Moses Jackson climb the cable of the Echo tower in the winter of 2000.

James McSheehy — Silver-Tongued Statesman

Big-city mayors are expected to fill many roles — politician, civic leader, and head of an extended family of residents of the fair city they represent. Mayor George Christopher was not only the city's chief executive but also owner of a dairy. Below, he receives a crown adorned with a Christopher milk carton from comedian Phyllis Diller. Opposite: Mayor Christopher, a baseball player himself in his youth, throws out the first ball at the very first National League game on the West Coast. The new San Francisco Giants beat the new Los Angeles Dodgers 8-0 on that day, April 15, 1958, at Seals Stadium.

James McSheehy, elected to the Board of Supervisors in 1918, served for twenty-four years. Here are a few of his famous pronouncements:

His advice to others: "We must put our shoulders to the wheel and push the ship of state up Market Street."

In opposing a building project: "This has all the earmarks of an eyesore."

On another project he thought too expensive: "This comes within a few pennies of being a very large sum."

He opposed equivocation: "You can't straddle the fence and still keep your ear to the ground."

He was outraged to learn that the Hetch Hetchy water project also included facilities for generation of electricity. "Do you mean to tell me," he thundered, "the people of San Francisco are drinking water after all the electricity has been removed from it?"

He once told a delegation that had come to his office: "Ladies, I have some figures which I want you to take home in your heads, which I know are concrete."

He defended his record: "I may have missed a committee meeting now and then and been late occasionally to our Monday meetings, but no one, sir, can say I've been incumbent."

"I am a candidate for mayor," he said in 1939, "but I haven't yet decided to run."

McSheehy did run and was defeated by Angelo J. Rossi — the incumbent.

ceeded by Judge Elmer E. Robinson, another friend of business.

GEORGE CHRISTOPHER: Greek-born owner of a dairy company and a popular supervisor, Christopher was elected mayor in 1955. Two distinctions: he brought the Giants to San Francisco, and he made friends with Nikita Khrushchev. In 1957, there were only sixteen major-league baseball teams, none of them west of Kansas City. Los Angeles civic leaders were trying secretly to lure the Brooklyn Dodgers to their city. Christopher got word of it and pulled off a double play: he talked the New York Giants into moving to San Francisco at the same time. When the Los Angeles Dodgers played the San Francisco Giants at Seals Stadium in 1958, Christopher was at the top of his game. (although a few locals did not take to the team from New York, and some even booed the great Willie Mays.) The next year, at the height of the Cold War, Soviet Premier Khrushchev visited the United States. He was received properly in Washington, D.C., but coolly in Manhattan, and he felt he had been insulted in Los Angeles and threatened to go home. But when Khrushchev got to San Francisco, Christopher treated him

Pedestrians walk across the
Golden Gate Bridge on May 27,
1937, the day before it opened.
Right: Today, the span towers
over Fort Point.
Opposite: The bridge takes
shape a year from completion.

Spanning the Golden Gate

It is difficult to imagine the Golden Gate Strait without the bridge. An Ansel Adams photograph of it, taken from the ocean, shows the long peninsula reaching out toward Marin, the gray strait in between, a mile wide. Army Captain John C. Fremont named it Chrysopylae, or Golden Gate, after the Golden Horn of Byzantium. Building a bridge across the Golden Gate once was thought to be impossible — the towers would have to be as high as a seventy-story building, the span between them 4,200 feet long. No one had ever built such a thing. But San Francisco did, in the slide-rule engineering days of the Depression.

There was a lot of opposition — more than 2,300 lawsuits were filed to block construction. The ferry and railroad people, who had a monopoly on transbay transportation, were against it, as was the Sierra Club on the grounds it would deface the Golden Gate. But the bridge, which cost twenty-seven million dollars and the lives of ten workers and opened to traffic on May 28, 1937, was a beauty. Even the men who worked on it knew it was special: "Sometimes I just go out and look at it," said bridge worker Ed Souza on the bridge's fiftieth birthday in 1987. "I don't think I'll ever get tired of it. It was the greatest job I ever had." Mac Silvert, an engineer, flew over the

Golden Gate in a plane before the cables were spun, when the towers stood alone. "By God, it was beautiful," he said. The man who gets the most credit for the bridge was Joseph Strauss, a bridge engineer who made the Golden Gate his life's work. Strauss was a promoter and visionary, but the actual design was by Charles Ellis, O.H. Amman and Leon Moisseiff. The idea for the red color of the bridge, it is said, came from Irving Morrow, an architect who thought the red primer the steel came with would grace the site. The color, it was decided, would be called "international orange." Strauss was enthusiastic. He said he was tired of "boring" gray bridges.

like an old pal. The two rode through the city in a limo, and Khrushchev, noticing people waving at him, leaned far out of the window to wave back. Christopher pulled him back in. "If you fall out of the car," the mayor said, "nobody in the world will believe I didn't push you." Khrushchev laughed hard. San Francisco crowds applauded the Soviet leader, to his delight. "This is the damnedest city," said New York newspaper editor Frank Conniff. "They cheer Khrushchev, and they boo Willie Mays."

JOSEPH L. ALIOTO: A brilliant antitrust lawyer who could wheel and deal and write poetry, he succeeded former U.S. Representative John F. Shelley as mayor in 1968. The look of modern San Francisco is his legacy. He was a tireless promoter of downtown growth — the Embarcadero Center, the Transamerica Pyramid, and dozens of other high-rises were constructed on his watch. Developers and construction unions liked Alioto; environmentalists and political progressives disliked what they called "the Manhattanization" of San Francisco. His regime was marked by high-profile lawsuits, and in his second term, he was found in violation of the city's conflict-of-interest law in a case involving his fam-

Opposite: In one of the eternal rites of spring, Mayor Joseph Alioto throws out the first ball at opening day at Candlestick Park, April 12, 1971, before a well-dressed crowd.
Above: Alioto, ever the showman, joins *Chronicle* columnist Herb Caen in July 1968 to dedicate a new radio antenna in the Broadway Tunnel. For years, Caen (third from right) had complained that his car radio went dead in the tunnel — once while he was listening to a tense Giants game. Sailors on the aircraft carrier *Coral Sea*, based in Alameda, installed wires to allow reception inside.

1939 — A Dream of Peace and Progress

The Golden Gate International Exposition, celebrating the completion of two great bridges, was built on an artificial island atop a shoal north of Yerba Buena Island. About 287,000 tons of boulders and millions of cubic yards of sand and gravel were dumped into the bay to create a four-hundred-acre space named Treasure Island. Opened in 1939, the fair seemed a fitting climax to a decade that had begun with the Depression and ended with the construction of two engineering marvels.

The fair was capped by the four-hundred-foot Tower of the Sun, designed by Arthur Brown Jr., architect of San Francisco City Hall. The rest of the buildings were a combination of Art Deco architecture and Mayan and Cambodian themes, a new style intended to represent the Pacific Basin. All of it was done in sun-washed colors, lit softly at night. To *Chronicle* columnist Herb Caen, it was "a place of lightness and brightness filled with magic fountains and far-off music."

The fair was supposed to represent the future, and it did. Big seaplanes called Flying Clippers took off from the Treasure Island Lagoon bound for Hawaii, Midway, Guam, and Manila, part of the recently inaugurated transpacific air service. Another big hit was a new entertainment medium called television, using a technique invented in San Francisco by Philo T. Farnsworth. And at Sally Rand's Nude Ranch, young women clad in cowboy hats and little else posed prettily for the customers. In 1939, a million visitors came to the Bay Area and spent forty-three million dollars.

The future did not turn out as the fair planners imagined. They had thought Treasure Island would become San Francisco's airport, but when America went to war, the US Navy took over the island, tore down the Tower of the Sun and all but a handful of buildings, and turned the site into a drab military base. The city got Treasure Island back in 1996.

Opposite: Governor Frank Merriam breaks ground for the buildings on the brand-new Treasure Island in 1936. The exposition will include pavilions from many foreign countries, and flags of seventy-eight nations, including Japan and Nazi Germany, are on display at the ceremony. When World War II broke out in September 1939, the realities of the time overshadowed the fair's optimistic view of the future. At top is the Tower of the Sun; at left is an amusement zone called the Gayway; at right is Willie, the Westinghouse robot.

ily-owned shipping line and the Port of San Francisco; he managed to avoid prosecution.

GEORGE MOSCONE: State Senator Moscone barely squeaked by conservative Supervisor John Barbagelata in the fall of 1975, but his election marked a sea change in San Francisco politics. Moscone, an old-school native San Franciscan, was elected by a coalition of voters who felt left out of City Hall — minorities, gays, and others who formed what they called a progressive alliance, which has dominated San Francisco politics ever since. Moscone's administration opened the doors. Camera shop owner Harvey Milk ran for supervisor in 1977. "Once the first gay is elected to the board," he said, "it will never be an issue again." He was right. Dan White, who had been a police officer and a firefighter, also was elected, saying he represented the old San Francisco. He was a brooding and angry man, and when he quit the board in a fit of pique and Moscone refused to reappoint him, he sneaked into City Hall and assassinated both Moscone and Milk on November 27, 1978.

DIANNE FEINSTEIN: The president of the Board of Supervisors on that fateful November day in

Opposite: State Senator George Moscone hugs his wife, Gina, at an election-night celebration on November 4, 1975. Moscone finished first in a three-candidate race, conservative Supervisor John Barbagelata ran second, and Supervisor Dianne Feinstein was third. Moscone was elected in the December runoff against Barbagelata, but he was assassinated along with Supervisor Harvey Milk three years later.
Above: Moscone's funeral procession leaves St. Mary's Cathedral. Feinstein, who became mayor, recalled: "He used to say he was the luckiest guy in the world to be mayor of the greatest city in the world."

Above: One of Dianne
Feinstein's achievements was
rebuilding the ancient and
neglected cable car system
— a project that cost sixty-four
million dollars and took two
years to complete. Here she
rides one of the newly
refurbished cars in 1984 along
with singer Tony "I Left My
Heart in San Francisco" Bennett.
At right: Feinstein's time as
mayor begins on a somber note
as she leads the Board
of Supervisors in a silent prayer
for George Moscone and
Harvey Milk and their families
and friends at the first
board meeting after the assassi-
nations. Feinstein, who had been
president of the board, got a lot
of credit for leading the city
through difficult times.

1978, Feinstein heard the shots and found Milk's body. In a solemn voice, she announced that the mayor and the supervisor had been assassinated. She became mayor and she held the city together in the dark winter that followed the murders and the Jonestown massacre. She later won election in her own right and put her stamp on San Francisco. A centrist, Feinstein ran the city as if she were its CEO. When the cable car system was discovered to be on the verge of collapse from years of deferred maintenance, she had it rebuilt with federal and private money. She opened up city government to women. Feinstein later ran unsuccessfully for governor, then was elected a U.S. senator.

WILLIE BROWN: Feinstein was followed by Art Agnos, who lost his re-election bid to ex-police chief Frank Jordan, who in turn lost to Brown in 1995. Willie L. Brown Jr. was a veteran member of the state Assembly who had reigned as the all-powerful speaker for years before a term-limit law forced him out. Dapper, stylish, a political pro to his fingertips, Brown ran the city as if he were an elected grand duke. Brown's politics, his friends, and the favors he dispensed often were controversial, but no one ever

Top: Trailing in pre-election polls, Mayor Frank Jordan (right) allows Los Angeles disc jockeys Mark Thompson and Brian Phelps to join him in the shower in October 1995. Jordan explained that he was "squeaky clean" with "nothing to hide." Unimpressed, voters replaced him with outgoing Assembly Speaker Willie Brown, above.

proved he had done anything illegal. An attorney who fought civil rights battles in the city in the '60s, Brown liked to say he was only a poor kid from Mineola, Texas, but in fact he was urbane and a great admirer of the city's past. San Francisco changed a great deal during his administrations: a new baseball park was built on the waterfront, the Embarcadero was turned into a grand promenade, and the City Hall building, which had been damaged in the 1989 Loma Prieta earthquake, was restored to a glittering jewel. Brown, who served two terms, was mayor during the high-flying dot-com boom.

GAVIN NEWSOM: The youngest mayor in nearly a century, Newsom came from a well-connected family that had arrived in San Francisco in 1855. Handsome as a movie star and derided by his foes on the left as a lightweight, Newsom surprised the city in the first days of his administration in 2004 by paying attention to neglected neighborhoods, getting tough on crime, and working hard to solve the city's homelessness problem. In February 2004, he amazed the country by directing city officials to allow same-sex marriages, sparking a passionate national debate.

Opposite: Mayor Willie L. Brown Jr. sings a tune from *The Lion King* at Beach Blanket Babylon's twenty-fifth anniversary gala in June 1999. Brown, who ruled with an iron hand, was only half-kidding about the crown and the regal robes.
Above: Brown's successor, Gavin Newsom, shocked the nation in 2004 by ordering city officials to issue marriage licenses to same-sex couples. Here he poses with Cissie Bonini (left) and Lora Pertle at their City Hall wedding reception.

Clockwise from left: Governor Edmund G. "Pat" Brown, former San Francisco district attorney, holds *The San Francisco Chronicle* with a headline on his 1958 election as governor; the Rev. Cecil Williams of Glide Memorial Church in 1980; Vincent Hallinan, noted leftist lawyer, his wife, Vivian, and their son, Terence, later San Francisco district attorney, in 1959.

Movers and Shakers

Many influential San Franciscans have helped make the city great. A small sample:

A.P. Giannini founded Bank of Italy, which became Bank of America … **Henry Doelger** built homes on former sand dunes in what became the Sunset district … **The Flood family** got its money from Nevada silver mines; current prince: **James C. Flood** … **Chuck Williams** founded Williams-Sonoma stores … **Ray Dolby**, the sound guy … **Susie Tompkins Buell**, cofounder of Esprit clothing … **Ben Swig** owned the Fairmont Hotel … **The Haas family**, major philanthropists and descendants of Levi Strauss, run the clothing company … **Charles Schwab**, discount brokerage founder … financiers **Warren Hellman** and **Charles Crocker** … **Louis Lurie**, capitalist, and son **Bob**, owner of real estate and, once, the Giants … **Charles Howard**, owned racehorse Seabiscuit … **Gordon Getty**, billionaire arts patron … **Carole Shorenstein Hays**, stage impresario … **Alma de Bretteville Spreckels** gave the city the Palace of the Legion of Honor … **Walter Shorenstein**, power behind many thrones … **Richard Goldman**, insurance

broker and environmental prize benefactor ... **Howard Gossage**, visionary advertising executive ... **Cyril Magnin**, merchant prince ... **David Brower**, founder of Friends of the Earth ... attorney **Eva Paterson**, who helped open police and fire departments to minorities and women; defense lawyer **Jake Ehrlich**, called "The Master" in '40s and '50s; politically connected attorney **William Coblentz** ... **Warren Bechtel**, founder of global construction company later led by son **Stephen Sr.** and grandson **Stephen Jr.** ... **Mimi Silbert** built Delancey Street Foundation ... **Carleton Goodlett** and **Thomas Fleming** of the *African American Sun-Reporter* ... **Mona Lisa Yuchengco**, founder, *Filipinas* magazine ... **Kevin Starr**, historian ... **Harold Gilliam**, environmental writer ... **Halsey Minor**, CNET founder ... **Fremont Older**, crusading newspaper editor in '06 ... **Vic and Tony Morabito**, founders of the 49ers ... **Franklin Mieuli** brought the Warriors to town ... **Peter Magowan**, owner of the Giants ... Nobel Prize winners in medicine **Herbert Boyer** ('73), **J. Michael Bishop**, **Harold Varmus** ('89), and **Stanley Prusiner** ('97) ... Filipino community leader **Rodel Rodis** ... attorney, banker, insurance executive **Chung Wing Chan**.

Clockwise from top left: Semanticist, San Francisco State College President and U.S. Senator S.I. Hayakawa; city protocol chief Charlotte Maillard Shultz in 1980; Philip Burton, political power broker who, like his brother John, served in the state Legislature and US Congress; *Chronicle* founder M.H. de Young; Craig Newmark of Craigslist; flamboyant attorney Melvin Belli.

PART SIX

The Big Story

I f you come to San Francisco, don't put a flower in your hair. Put a pencil behind your ear and a notebook in your pocket and bring a camera. This is a hell of a town for news. Always has been.

On a beautiful October day in 1989, an earthquake rocked the Bay Area. More than sixty people died, five when brick walls collapsed on Bluxome Street in the South of Market area.

San Francisco has seen earthquakes, fires, riots, strikes, celebrations, kidnappings, murders, triumphs, and tragedies. San Francisco's biggest earthquake, one hundred years ago, nearly destroyed the city. The next quake — the Little Big One, they called it — happened just as the San Francisco Giants were about to play the Oakland Athletics in the 1989 World Series. It would be hard to top that one for timing.

But the real story is always just beneath the surface, like an underground stream. The real story in San Francisco is constant change. A disaster was followed by more than twenty years of good times, followed by a bleak Depression marked by strikes and riots, followed by the opening of two world-famous bridges.

World War II transformed the city, turning it into a staging area for millions of soldiers, sailors, and

Wearing a bow tie, a bowler hat, and a confident smile, political boss Abe Ruef arrives at San Francisco's temporary courthouse at the Temple Sherith Israel on California Street early in 1907 to stand trial on bribery and corruption charges. Ruef, forty-three at the time, held no office but ran the city through the Union Labor Party's ticket of crooked city officials, headed by Mayor Eugene Schmitz. A sensational series of trials that went on for a year showed that the mayor and the entire Board of Supervisors were on the take. But only Ruef paid the price; he served nearly five years in San Quentin State Prison. After his release, he had an office in the Columbus Tower, and the sign on his door said: "A. Ruef. Ideas, Investments, and Real Estate."
Below: President Warren Harding, taken ill on a cross-country trip, died in the city's Palace Hotel in 1923.

Marines. After the war, thousands of new people came west, and the city's pretty suburbs became cities in their own right. The Bay Area's old industrial base faded, but new industries of ideas and technology emerged. San Francisco's political scene, which once featured bitter — and sometimes bloody — clashes between working people and an entrenched business establishment, shifted as well, and "San Francisco" became code for liberal politics.

Sometimes, the changes were like a parade, a pageant moving along Market Street.

In 1906, refugees made their way down Market, carrying all they had left, fleeing disaster.

In 1916, a Market Street parade was bombed by terrorists who were never caught. Two years later, the doughboys marched up Market, back from World War I.

In 1934, union workers moved up Market in a solemn, silent parade to mourn their dead, killed by police.

When World War II was over, the celebration on Market Street turned into a drunken riot. The

Police interview witnesses after a bomb at Market and Steuart streets interrupted the Preparedness Day parade on July 22, 1916, killing ten people and injuring more than forty. Labor activists Tom Mooney and Warren Billings were framed for the crime and served twenty years in prison. Below: Watched by thousands of spectators around the bay, the China Clipper soars over the Golden Gate Bridge, then under construction, on November 22, 1935, bound for Honolulu and eventually Manila, inaugurating the first regular air service between the West Coast and Asia.

Crowds gather in downtown San Francisco to snap up newspaper extras describing the attack on Pearl Harbor. Suddenly, the United States was at war, and the West Coast was in a panic. Rumors spread that a Japanese fleet lurked outside the Golden Gate and that spies and saboteurs were everywhere. Early in December, the Army announced that Japanese planes had flown over the city. Despite air raid alarms, San Francisco glowed with light, and a furious General John DeWitt went to City Hall the next day to chew out top officials. Mayor Angelo Rossi was unimpressed: "No bombs fell, did they?"

riot was forgotten when the soldiers, home from the war, marched up the street later in 1945.

Shriners and Elks paraded, as did native sons, Irishmen in green, Chinese with paper lions and dragons a block long, veterans of the nation's wars, gay activists, the new San Francisco Giants, and the homegrown 49ers. Protests tied up Market Street — people sat down and refused to move, or attacked stores, or simply walked up the street by the thousands, carrying signs. In the second half of the century, anti-war demonstrations drew tens of thousands of protesters.

A century of people cheered victories, mourned deaths, protested, and celebrated, moving up and down Market Street like a river.

Early in 1942, General DeWitt, commanding Army forces from San Francisco's Presidio, became convinced that people of Japanese descent on the West Coast were a threat. Thousands of Japanese American families were moved to internment camps far from their Pacific Coast homes. Many were forced to sell all they had at ruinous prices. Below, Dorothea Lange photographed students reciting the Pledge of Allegiance at Raphael Weill (now Rosa Parks) Elementary School weeks before the Japanese Americans among them were shipped to camps.

Sailors on San Francisco's
Market Street celebrate peace
by kissing any woman they
can find after Japan announced
in 1945 that it would accept
surrender terms to end
World War II.

At right: While the war still
rages, President Harry Truman
speaks to representatives
of fifty nations meeting at the
War Memorial Opera House
to shape a charter for a
new world organization —
the United Nations.

VICTORY EXTRA!
San Francisco Chronicle

PEACE!

Allied Troops Told to Cease Firing; Enemy Gets Orders for Surrender

International delegates creating the United Nations meet in the Opera House in April 1945. They signed the organization's charter on June 26.

At left: Meanwhile, there were still scores to settle. Iva Toguri D'Aquino, who was born in Los Angeles, arrives in federal court in San Francisco in 1948 to stand trial for treason. The charge: that she was "Tokyo Rose," who broadcast for the Japanese in World War II. Convicted and sent to prison, she was released in 1956 and was pardoned by President Gerald Ford in 1977.

San Francisco has always been a place where citizens take to the streets to protest the status quo. Above: Students and other young people demonstrate at City Hall against the House Un-American Activities Committee meeting there in 1960. The protesters are both angry and wet — they have been driven back by police using fire hoses. At left: Women protest hiring and promotion policies at a department store stockholders' meeting on Nob Hill in the 1970s. At right: Pickets from the Congress of Racial Equality march for civil rights in front of Lincoln's statue at City Hall in May 1963.

The old Sutro Baths, a favorite of San Franciscans since the 1890s, goes up in flames in the summer of 1966. The baths at one time had a skating rink, several swimming pools, and a museum of curiosities on the cliffs above the ocean. Sightseers can still view the ruins.

At left: Another San Francisco favorite, dancer Carol Doda, shows off her newly silicone-enhanced breasts at a press conference in July 1965. Doda introduced topless dancing to the city in the summer of 1964. During the same week, the Republicans nominated Barry Goldwater for president at the Cow Palace.

It was billed as a great moment in the history of the world — June 21, 1967, the summer solstice, the official beginning of San Francisco's Summer of Love. Above, thousands of celebrants gather in Golden Gate Park. For several years thereafter, the young came to San Francisco from everywhere, wearing flowers in their hair, dancing and singing and smoking, talking about peace and love. These flower children attracted worldwide attention.

A party of seventy-eight Indians landed on Alcatraz Island in San Francisco Bay in November 1969 and claimed the island for Indians of all tribes. The federal prison on the island had been closed in 1963 and the land declared surplus, but the Indians demanded it as a cultural center. At first, the US Coast Guard imposed a blockcade, and Indians got supplies from yachts like the one above. After nineteen months, the occupation drifted into violence and chaos, and government agents removed the occupants. Today Alcatraz is part of a national park.

The late '60s and early '70s were an angry time.
At left: Attorney Terence Hallinan was injured in a scuffle with police at a 1968 sit-in at San Francisco State College. (Hallinan later became district attorney of San Francisco, and the college became a university.)
Below: Anti-war demonstrators sit down to protest the Vietnam War in the City Hall rotunda in May 1970.
Below right: Police push back anti-war demonstrators on Nob Hill in December 1970.

Newspaper heiress Patricia Hearst was kidnapped by terrorists calling themselves the Symbionese Liberation Army in 1974. In one of the strangest cases in Bay Area history, Hearst later helped rob a San Francisco bank, was convicted of the crime, and served time in prison. Released in 1979, right, she shows off a T-shirt given to her by bodyguard Bernard Shaw, whom she later married. Eventually, she was pardoned.

President Gerald Ford ducks as a shot fired by self-styled radical Sara Jane Moore whizzes over his head outside the St. Francis Hotel on September 22, 1975. At right: In a letter to *The Chronicle*, the mysterious killer who called himself the Zodiac taunts police by describing his crimes to the news media. He killed as many as five people in 1968 and '69, but the case never has been solved.

Dear Editor
 This is the Zodiac speaking I am back with you. Tell herb caen I am here, I have always been here. That city pig toschi is good·but I am ~bu~ smarter and better he will get tired then leave me alone. I am waiting for a good movie about me. who will play me. I am now in control of all things.
 Yours truly :
 ⊕ - guess

SFPD - O

In the early 1970s, a charismatic preacher named Jim Jones, at left, took over an old synagogue in San Francisco's Western Addition for his Peoples Temple. Jones and his flock were politically active, helping liberal causes and politicians like new Mayor George Moscone, who appointed Jones to the city Housing Commission. But tales of strange and evil behavior started to circulate about Jones and his church, and Jones took hundreds of followers to a jungle settlement in Guyana that he named Jonestown. When U.S. Representative Leo Ryan of San Mateo flew there to investigate in November 1978, church gunmen killed him and four others. The story took an even more tragic turn when Jones ordered the residents of Jonestown to drink fruit punch laced with poison. When it was over, more than nine hundred had died, including Jones.

November 1978 was a dark
month in San Francisco. Only
days after the deaths in
Jonestown, Mayor George
Moscone and Supervisor Harvey
Milk (shaking hands in photo
opposite) were assassinated by
Dan White, a former police
officer who had been elected to
the Board of Supervisors the
year before.

Milk, shown opposite at top left
riding in the gay pride parade,
was a Castro district camera
store owner who was elected to
the board in 1977, becoming
the first openly gay elected
official in San Francisco. White,
a bitter and unstable man, quit
the board in October but then
changed his mind. He went to
Moscone's City Hall office and
asked the mayor to reappoint
him. When Moscone refused,
White shot him, reloaded his
pistol, went to Milk's office, and
killed the supervisor as well. At
left: White is taken to jail after
his arrest later the same day.
That night, a huge crowd,
singing, praying, and carrying
candles, marched from the
Castro to City Hall. In the
spring, White was convicted
of manslaughter, not murder,
and another crowd, this time
an angry one, marched on City
Hall. Protesters burned police
cars and attacked the building
in what became known as the
White Night riot. Released
from prison in 1984, White
later killed himself.

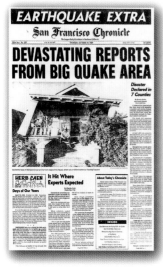

October 17, 1989: History is being made in San Francisco, but it's not what the city expected. It is the third game of the Bay Bridge World Series — the first ever between San Francisco and Oakland. At 5:04 p.m., just before the game was to start at Candlestick Park, an earthquake rocked the Bay Area. One person died when a section of the Bay Bridge fell (opposite below and at left) and many more when the Nimitz Freeway collapsed in Oakland. Others died in Santa Cruz and Watsonville. Parts of San Francisco's Marina district were badly damaged, including a three-story apartment house that pancaked (above). Everything residents had left — including a bicycle and a surfboard (opposite top) — had to be removed.

The turbulent '90s: Conflict in the far-off Middle East provoked protests in San Francisco.
At right: Demonstrators, angry about the U.S.-led bombing of Iraq in the Gulf War in January 1991, set fire to a California Highway Patrol car near the Bay Bridge.
Below right: Eleven years later, in 2002, the situation in Iraq heated up again, and Market Street is filled curb-to-curb with demonstrators in front of the Ferry Building tower.
Below: American forces invaded Iraq in March 2003, producing more protests; despite police restraints, a demonstrator manages to give the peace sign.

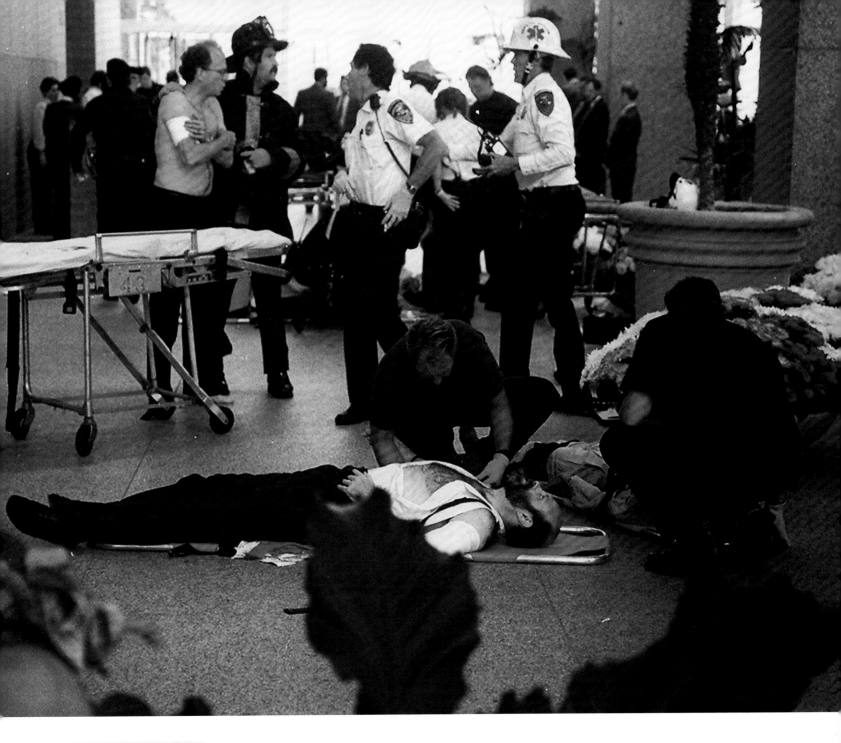

On a hot afternoon in the beginning of summer 1993, Gian Luigi Ferri, a loner with a seething resentment of lawyers, walked into the Pettit & Martin law offices at 101 California Street and began shooting. He carried automatic weapons, and when he was finished, eight people were dead and six others wounded. Then he killed himself. At right: The dot-com boom was almost like a gold rush in the San Francisco of the 1990s — for a while, you could even access the Internet in a taxi.

The Rainbow's End

When Del Martin grew up in San Francisco, she didn't know any lesbians. "Years ago, nobody dared to come out," she said. "We lost so much by it … family, friends, sometimes your liberty." She met Phyllis Lyon in Seattle in 1950, moved back to San Francisco soon afterward. In 2004, these lesbian-rights matriarchs were married on Valentine's Day in Mayor Gavin Newsom's office in City Hall in the first of thousands of same-sex weddings. To conservatives around the country, that was proof that San Francisco was out of step with the rest of the nation. To San Franciscans, it was no great surprise. The city's emergence as a haven for gays and lesbians is one of the major events of the last century.

Homosexuals, of course, have always lived in San Francisco, although gays and lesbians kept a low profile. Author Armistead Maupin wrote that gay people were "the world's most invisible population." For good reason: homosexual acts were illegal in California until 1975, when state legislators repealed the law prohibiting sodomy between consenting adults. San Francisco Assemblyman Willie Brown had

STOP ATTACKS
ON LESBIANS & GAYS

Opposite, above: San Francisco was amazed when thousands of people showed up for the gay freedom parade in 1972 (shown here at Civic Center). A generation later, the parade was the city's largest. Opposite, below: Sweet Pam, John Rothermel, and Pristine Condition of the Cockettes in 1972. Above: Police and gay activists clash at City Hall during the White Night riot in May 1979. At left: Dressed in leathers and carrying festive balloons, participants wait for the 1981 freedom parade to start.

By the mid-'80s, the AIDS epidemic was decimating the city's gay community. The memorial quilt, with hundreds of names of the dead, goes on display at Moscone Center in 1987.
Opposite, above: Dr. William Owen examines AIDS patient Fred Hoffman at St. Luke's Hospital in 1987 while Russ Fields, Hoffman's partner, provides moral support.
Opposite, below left: The Sisters of Perpetual Indulgence celebrate the Fourth of July 2002 at Dolores Park.
Opposite, below right: A pink triangle is displayed on Twin Peaks during pride week, while a rainbow flag flies at Castro and Market streets.

to introduce the repeal bill five times before finally it passed by a single vote.

The city's gay population began to grow after World War II, when many gay men who had passed through the Bay Area in the military felt the pull of the West, finding a place of beauty where their privacy would be respected. Gays came to a city with a reputation for tolerance and an attitude to match at a time when the economic and social climate was just right. "They didn't want as a gay guy to go back to the Middle West," said Ken Maley, a consultant active in the gay community. Not long after the war, the Beat generation flourished in San Francisco, and gays enjoyed the bohemian lifestyle. By the '60s, a lively gay life sprang up along Polk Street — but gay bars and other meeting places often were raided by police. The Tavern Guild, the first gay business association in the country, started in 1962 to deal with police harassment. Police raided a New Year's costume party at the California Hall, just a block from City Hall, on Jan. 1, 1965, outraging gays and leading the ACLU and others to take up the cause of gay rights for the first time. The 1969 Stonewall riots in New York City, in which gays fought back against the po-

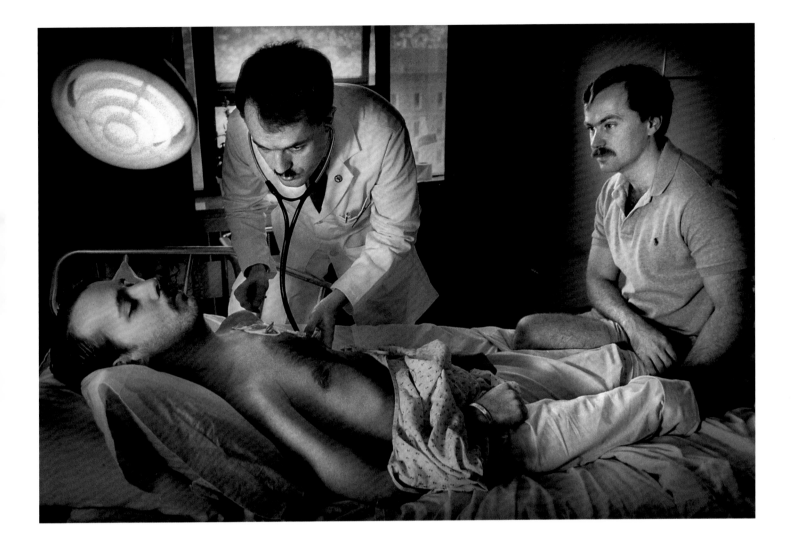

Gay and lesbian marriages took center stage at City Hall on Valentine's Day weekend 2004. Phyllis Lyon (left) and Del Martin, the city's premier lesbian couple — they've been together fifty-one years — are married in the mayor's office on February 12.
Opposite: Among the other thousands of couples married that weekend are Eric Ethington (left) and Doug Okun. They brought their twin daughters and were declared "spouses for life" by Marriage Commissioner Richard Ow.

lice, marked another turning point. And in June 1970 on Polk Street, gays staged the first gay rights march in San Francisco. Perhaps thirty people participated; more came to a "gay-in" in Golden Gate Park the next day. Two years later, a Stonewall riots commemoration in the city drew fifty thousand people. By 1973, the annual Stonewall parade had become the Gay Freedom Day parade; by 1975, it drew eighty thousand people; by 1978, 350,000. Today, the gay pride parade draws nearly twice that many.

Several factors led to the growth of the gay rights movement. Back in the late '60s and early '70s, gays, women, and minorities were riding a wave of social change in the country — civil rights, sexual liberation, feminism, protests against the Vietnam War. San Francisco was on the cutting edge of change. In 1969, a gifted young man named Sylvester James came to San Francisco "to live his dream," said *Chronicle* music critic Joel Selvin. Sylvester, who used only his first name, was a member of the Cockettes, a troupe of post-hippie, pansexual entertainers whose outrageous act drew large audiences. "They expanded reality," said Strange de Jim, who wrote the book *San Francisco's Castro*. Around that time,

de Jim wrote, the blue-collar neighborhood called Eureka Valley was being transformed into the Castro as jobs vanished with the decline of the city's port and manufacturing base. The younger generation was moving to the suburbs, and older residents, born and raised in the city, were dying off. "Property values dropped when the blue-collar jobs left, and that's when gay people moved in," de Jim said. It was classic gentrification with a San Francisco twist. The Castro suddenly was not your father's Eureka Valley.

For a while, gay life in San Francisco was like riding a skyrocket, like being at a wild party without rules. "It was an open town," said writer Frank Robinson. "There was a lot of sexual tension." Gays developed a political base, and in 1977, Harvey Milk, a gay Castro Street camera store owner, became the first openly gay person elected to San Francisco's Board of Supervisors. But the story had an aura of Greek tragedy: Milk and Mayor George Moscone, who had opened city government to groups previously excluded, were shot to death in City Hall in 1978 by Supervisor Dan White, a former police officer and firefighter who claimed to represent the city's old values. After that, nothing was the same. White was convicted of manslaughter

Figures from the wedding cake of seventy-eight-year-old Otis Charles, the first openly gay Episcopal bishop in the country, and Felipe Sanchez Paris on April 24, 2004.

instead of murder, and hundreds of gays and others rioted, smashing the ornate glass doors at City Hall, looting nearby stores, and burning several police cars in what became known as the White Night riot.

Then came AIDS, a disease first reported in the mainstream media in 1982. A total of 330 cases was reported in *The Chronicle* that year. "In 1981 and '82 it really took off. It was terrifying," Robinson said. "It was brutal. It was like a war. There were twenty thousand casualties in San Francisco."

Today, outside the Castro, particularly along Cortland Avenue in Bernal Heights, a lesbian community thrives. Gays and lesbians are in every part of city life: as police officers, firefighters, judges, supervisors, and state legislators, in music, the arts, and business, everywhere in San Francisco. No big deal.

"It was the big gay experiment in San Francisco; a group of people that had been fenced out, and they found a way to get through the fence," Maley said. "They used their political and economic power to get access to City Hall, to lead gay lives, to win the right to marry. I think it turned out pretty well."

**Ordinary scenes
in San Francisco:
Opposite, a woman named
Fish (left) and her girlfriend,
Sidney Carr, pause with their
bike in the gay pride parade
of 2000.
Above, two men go out
on a date in the Castro
in the spring of 1999.**

Hometown Heroes

The 49ers were San Francisco's first big-league team — and most successful, winning five Super Bowls. At left, the great wide receiver Jerry Rice breaks loose against the San Diego Chargers in the '95 Super Bowl. The Niners won 49-26.

Sometimes, late at night, when the air is still, they say you can hear cheers from the games of long ago, very faintly, the way you sometimes hear the ocean: thousands of voices shouting, yelling, booing, cheers for victory, the sour sound of defeat, hanging in the air.

The old baseball crowd gathered at the ramshackle Recreation Park at Fifteenth and Valencia streets in the Mission to cheer hometown heroes Ping Bodie (a North Beach kid whose real name was Francesco Pezzolo); Harry Heilmann (he won the American League batting title in 1923 with a .403 average — Babe Ruth had .393); Willie Kamm; Frankie Crosetti; Paul "Big Poison" Waner; and Joe Cronin. Seals Stadium was built in 1931 and for twenty-seven years was the city's baseball park and the best stadium in the minor leagues. All three DiMaggio brothers — Vince, Dom, and Joe — played for the Seals. Joe, the most famous, made his professional debut there Oct. 1, 1932, and the next year hit in sixty-one consecutive Pacific Coast League games while earning $225 a month. He left for New York

The legendary Joe DiMaggio was born in Martinez and raised in North Beach, and his road to the big leagues began with the San Francisco Seals of the Pacific Coast League. In 1933, DiMaggio (taking a swing in Seals Stadium, above), hit in sixty-one consecutive PCL games, a record that still stands. In 1936, he joined the New York Yankees.

Opposite: DiMaggio and Marilyn Monroe wait in a judge's chambers before their wedding at San Francisco City Hall in 1954. San Francisco was always close to DiMaggio's heart. He kept a home in the city, and his funeral was at Saints Peter and Paul Church in North Beach.

after the 1935 season, and the rest is history. Five-time American League All Star Ferris Fain said the '46 Seals were the best team he had ever played on. The '46 Seals, with Lefty O'Doul at the helm, drew 653,923 fans, a minor-league record that stood for nearly thirty years.

April 15, 1958, was a standing-ovation kind of day, and historic, too. The San Francisco Giants beat the Los Angeles Dodgers 8-0 at Seals Stadium in the first major-league game on the West Coast. It sounded as if a million people were there, but the park held just over twenty-three thousand. Out in Golden Gate Park stood Kezar Stadium, built in 1925 for high school and college football. In the leather-helmet days of the '30s and '40s, Sundays belonged to St. Mary's College, the University of Santa Clara, and the University of San Francisco. The greatest college all-star game — the East-West Shrine Game — was played at Kezar every winter. Big games drew fifty-eight thousand fans, sometimes even for high school matchups.

The best college team of all probably was USF's 1951 squad, undefeated, untied — and uninvited

to any bowl game. The Dons' fullback Ollie Matson, all-city at Washington High and all-everything at City College, was the leading ground-gainer in the country that year. But Matson and teammate Burl Toler were African American, and none of the big bowl games, then based in the segregated South, would invite USF unless the team left the two men home. The team refused to play without them. It was a terrific team: nine of the players went on to pro football, and three of them — Matson, Gino Marchetti, and Bob St. Clair — are in the Pro Football Hall of Fame.

The 49ers started up in 1946 and were an immediate hit — homegrown, home-owned, and San Francisco's first major-league team in any sport. San Franciscans cheered Frankie Albert, the elusive quarterback; Joe "The Toe" Vetrano; and later the famous "million-dollar backfield" — Y.A. Tittle, Hugh "The King" McElhenny, Joe "The Jet" Perry, and John Henry Johnson. Team owners paid a million bucks a year — real money in the '50s — for four backs. Kezar was famous for its hard-drinking fans. When they didn't like a 49ers player, they threw empty beer bottles at him. When they didn't like an

Opposite: For the first half of the twentieth century, baseball in San Francisco meant the Seals. The team had some great moments — one of them on Mother's Day 1953, when an irate Sadie Case of Emeryville came out of the stands to offer her glasses to the umpire so he could better see what he was calling.
Above: Francis "Lefty" O'Doul, longtime Seals manager, stands atop the dugout with two young fans in 1939.

The old Seals Stadium stands at Sixteenth and Bryant streets, where the Mission district meets Potrero Hill. Built in 1931, it served for twenty-seven years as the home of the minor-league Seals and was considered the best stadium in the league. The 1946 Seals, under manager Lefty O'Doul, drew more than 650,000 fans, a minor-league record that stood for more than thirty years. It was here on April 15, 1958, that the San Francisco Giants beat the Los Angeles Dodgers 8-0 in the first major-league game played on the West Coast. The Giants played here for two years before moving to windy Candlestick Park at the far end of town.

opposing coach, they ran out in the field and kicked him in the pants.

Kezar Pavilion, just around the corner, hosted USF's amazing basketball team. With Bill Russell and K.C. Jones, the Dons won two NCAA championships and sixty games in a row. From 1954 through 1958, they won 108 games and lost only ten.

Boxing, fueled with smoke and beer, flourished in San Francisco for decades. The biggest day: heavyweight champ Rocky Marciano knocked out Don Cockell in nine rounds at Kezar Stadium in May 1955. San Francisco had its own champs, such as Fred Apostoli, who rose from bellhop at the St. Francis Hotel to welterweight champion, and Carl "Bobo" Olson, from Hawaii but based in San Francisco. Olson fought Sugar Ray Robinson for the middleweight title at the Civic Auditorium in 1952 and lost, then won it in a decision against Randy Turpin in 1953. He defended his title twice in San Francisco but finally lost it in 1955 when Robinson knocked him out in the second round in Chicago.

Abe Attell, born in San Francisco in 1884, learned the fine art of boxing on the streets. At five-

In 1946, the Seals are the
hottest game in town,
and Phillip Baca stands
on Billy Davis's shoulders
to try to watch the show.
At left: An estimated
two hundred thousand people
turn out on April 14, 1958,
to welcome their new
San Francisco Giants, just
arrived from New York
and riding a parade
down Montgomery Street
the day before their first
game in the city.

Fans crowd the rooftops across the street from Kezar Stadium (above) as the 49ers face the Detroit Lions in the NFL Western Division playoff game on Dec. 22, 1957. The 49ers lost 31-27. The East-West Shrine college all-stars (at right, in 1965) also played at Kezar.

The old stadium, which could seat fifty-eight thousand and was famous for its fog and rowdy fans, was torn down and a smaller version rebuilt in the 1990s. In 2004, fans return to where it all started (left) to watch the 49ers scrimmage.

Opposite: The 49ers in 1960
had three quarterbacks
in preseason camp —
John Brodie (left) Bob Waters
and Y.A. Tittle. Brodie and
Tittle were stars.
Above, right: Stanford
All-American Frankie Albert
(above) was the first modern
T-formation quarterback
in the early 1940s and spent
seven years with the 49ers.
Above, left: USF's undefeated
1951 football team outscored
opponents by an average of 33-8
but was not invited to any bowl
games because Burl Toler
(front row, second from left)
and Ollie Matson (top row,
second from left) were black.
Nine team members went on
to play pro ball, five made NFL
all-star teams and three are
in the Pro Football Hall of Fame.
Pete Rozelle, the team's
publicity man, later became
commissioner of the NFL.

foot-four, he was world featherweight champ from 1901 to 1912. He is in the Boxing Hall of Fame, but

his name was sullied when he was accused of being the bagman for gamblers who fixed the 1919 World

Series, which the Chicago White Sox threw to the Cincinnati Reds. The starting pitcher for the Reds

in the first game was Dutch Ruether, who had played ball at St. Ignatius College — later called USF.

Another city star whose career was tainted was O.J. Simpson, born in San Francisco, raised in the

Potrero Hill projects, a football star at Galileo High School, a bigger star at City College. He won the

Heisman Trophy at USC and had a great pro career, but his fame came crashing down when he was

charged with murdering his ex-wife and her friend. After a sensational trial, he was acquitted.

Lincoln High produced world-class golfers, including US Open winners Ken Venturi and Johnny

Miller. Venturi won fourteen times on the PGA tour, while Miller won twenty-four times. Growing up

in San Francisco's brisk climate, Miller said, resulted in his one weakness — playing in humid weath-

er: "If it was 90 percent humidity, that was pretty much what I shot."

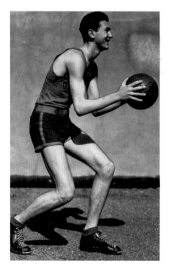

Golden Gate Park's tennis courts, built in 1901, produced two great female players, Rosie Casals and Alice Marble, both inducted into the International Tennis Hall of Fame. Casals, born in the city in 1948, earned twelve grand-slam doubles titles — seven with Billie Jean King. Marble, who held twelve US Open and six Wimbledon titles from 1936 to 1940, also played basketball, softball, and track at San Francisco Polytechnic High School. And she was the mascot for the Seals baseball team when she was thirteen, working out in practice with her hero, Joe DiMaggio.

The city can be a tough place for outdoor sports, as was discovered when a ballpark was built at windy Candlestick Point. Vice President Richard Nixon threw out the first ball of the 1960 season. Baseball was so hot and so new to the city that the air was filled with the tinny sound of transistor radios, tuned to Russ Hodges and Lon Simmons and the Giants. When the team hit a homer, Hodges called: "Bye-bye, baby!" The stars of those days were Willie Mays, Orlando Cepeda, Willie McCovey, and, on the mound, Juan Marichal. In the seventh game of the 1962 World Series against the Yankees, McCovey

Opposite, top: University
of San Francisco star Bill Russell
and teammates ride in a victory
parade on Montgomery Street
after winning the 1955 NCAA
basketball championship.
Opposite, below: San Francisco-
born Hank Luisetti, who played
for Galileo High in the city and
for Stanford, perfected the
one-hand shot and was the
first college player to score
50 points in a game.
At left: Russell and Cal's Bob
McKeen fight for the ball
at the Cow Palace in the Dons'
winning 1955 season. The Dons
led this game 20-0 and won it
by a score of 84-62. The team
won two national championships
and sixty games in a row and
had a 108-10 record
from 1954 to 1958.

hit a line drive in the ninth inning — the crowd rose to its feet, and then, God! right into the mitt of Bobby Richardson. The shouts of victory died in an instant. The Giants lost the series.

Meanwhile, after years of disappointment, great things happened at Candlestick Park in football season. The 49ers won the playoffs after the 1981 season in a famous game against the Dallas Cowboys and went on to win the Super Bowl. The 49ers teams of the '80s and early '90s were the best local teams ever, in any sport. Joe Montana, quarterbacking in four Super Bowls won by the Niners, was incomparable. Quarterback Steve Young, who was merely wonderful, led the team to a fifth Super Bowl victory in 1995. The 49er Faithful were in full cry in that old cement bowl — "Niners! Niners! Fooorty-Niners!" After the 49ers won championships, they rode up Market Street in triumph like conquering heroes as people stood on fire hydrants and leaned out of the windows of office buildings, roaring.

The worst day at Candlestick? The World Series, Giants against the Oakland Athletics, just after 5 p.m. on the warm, still afternoon of October 17, 1989, the third game of the Series about to begin,

Opposite: The Philadelphia Warriors moved to San Francisco in 1962, and that season, Wilt Chamberlain (number thirteen) averaged 44.6 points a game. But the team did not win, and Chamberlain was traded to the Philadelphia 76ers in 1965. The Warriors never got the arena they wanted; they moved to Oakland and changed their name to the Golden State Warriors in 1971. They won their only NBA championship in 1975 at the Cow Palace. Above: Carl "Bobo" Olson (at right) throws a right in one of his classic fights with Sugar Ray Robinson in San Francisco's Civic Auditorium in 1952. Olson lost this middleweight title bout.

Above, top: US Open champ Johnny Miller, a graduate of Lincoln High School, hits a fairway shot on the first hole of the Lake Merced Golf and Country Club in 1992.
Above: Alice Marble, who trained at Golden Gate Park tennis courts, held six Wimbledon and twelve US Open titles between 1936 and 1940. At right: Rosie Casals also trained at Golden Gate Park before winning twelve Grand Slam titles. Casals and Marble are in the International Tennis Hall of Fame.
Opposite: Ken Venturi explodes out of a trap en route to winning the city championship at Harding Park course in 1953. Venturi, a native San Franciscan and also a Lincoln grad, won the US Open in 1964. That year, he also was picked as *Sports Illustrated*'s Sportsman of the Year.

more than sixty thousand people in the park stirring in anticipation. You could hear a kind of rumble and then a gasp from the crowd. The stadium moved, the cement rippled, and the light towers swayed like trees in a wind. Earthquake! The Series resumed ten days later, and the A's won in a four-game sweep. The Giants moved out of Candlestick after the '99 season to the beautiful Pacific Bell Park (later renamed SBC Park), and amazing times followed. In 2001, Barry Bonds hit seventy-three home runs, more than anyone else in a single season. The World Series came to San Francisco in 2002, but the Giants lost again, this time to the Anaheim Angels. Bonds continued to assault the record books, although accusations (which he denied) that he had used steroids took off some luster.

In the summers of the twenty-first century, the sound that defines sports in the city comes from the crowd at SBC Park, standing and cheering, echoes bouncing off the shiny new condos, sounds rising and mixing with the faint echo of cheers long ago, when The San Francisco Century was young.

The Bay Area's Biggest Sports Moment

Candlestick Park, Sunday, January 10, 1982 – The 49ers are in the conference championship game against the Dallas Cowboys, who call themselves "America's Team" with the kind of Texas cockiness Californians dislike. Joe Montana is more their style – "Joe Cool," the ultimate quarterback.

The 49ers have had a wonderful year, thirteen wins, only three losses. But now they are behind, 27-21, with fifty-eight seconds to play. The 49ers are on the

Dallas six yard line, third down, three yards to go. This is the moment, and everybody knows it.

Montana goes back to pass, is flushed out of the pocket, throws the ball off his back foot. God, people thought, he's throwing the ball away.

Dwight Clark is in the back of the end zone. He thinks at first that the ball is too high. But as he leaps to catch it, his body stretched out, he realizes that this is the perfect pass. Nobody else can

catch it. Only Clark.

"It was a spectacular throw," Clark said later, "made under duress. It was thrown exactly where it needed to be thrown." He catches it, Ray Wersching kicks the extra point, and the 49ers win 28-27 to go to the Super Bowl.

It is The Catch. THE Catch, as if there were never any other.

The 49ers go on to win the Super Bowl against the Cincinnati Bengals. It is the first of five Super Bowl victories.

Coach Bill Walsh, Mayor Dianne
Feinstein and 49ers owner
Eddie DeBartolo ride in a victory
parade after the 1985
Super Bowl. The Niners beat
the Miami Dolphins 38-16.
At left: At Pat O'Shea's
Mad Hatter bar
in San Francisco's Richmond
district, fans celebrate the
winning touchdown in a third
Super Bowl victory, this time
in 1989 by a score of 20-16
against the Cincinnati Bengals.

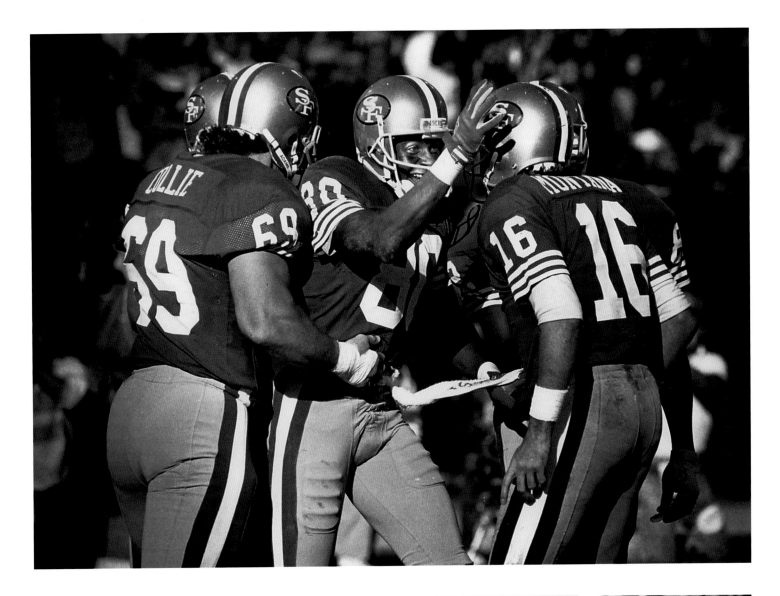

Great quarterbacks: Joe Montana (opposite) lifts arms in victory after a touchdown pass in the 1990 Super Bowl against the Denver Broncos; with Jerry Rice (number eighty) after an '89 playoff game; with family in Super Bowl parade, 1990. Above, Steve Young, who won a fifth Super Bowl, signals touchdown, 1998.

Opposite: The '60s were great years for the Giants. One reason was Willie McCovey, whose fearsome left-handed swing launched 521 home runs and put him in the Hall of Fame. Above: The Giants celebrate forcing a tie with the Dodgers in the 1962 pennant race. They won a three-game playoff, then lost to the Yankees in the seventh game of the World Series. At left: With the highest kick of any pitcher, Juan Marichal delivers in the '65 All-Star Game.

The most frightening moment in San Francisco sports: 5:04 p.m. October 17, 1989 — an earthquake hits just as the third game of the World Series is about to begin. Fans stayed for hours at Candlestick Park before the game was canceled. At right: Passing the torch: Willie Mays kisses his godson Barry Bonds as he gives him an Olympic Torch in honor of Bonds tying Mays's career-home-run record in 2004. Opposite: Mays swings for the fences in April 1958, at the peak of his career. Mays appeared in twenty-four All-Star games in his twenty-three years in the majors. The "Say Hey Kid" was a do-it-all superstar. He hit 660 home runs and had a lifetime .302 batting average. Pages 192-193: Bonds hit seventy-three home runs for the Giants — an all-time record — in 2001.

Creative City

Neal Cassady and Jack Kerouac
on Russian Hill in 1952.
In *On the Road*, Kerouac wrote
of his first look at "the
fabulous white city . . .
on her eleven mystic hills."

S an Francisco always has been schizophrenic: beautiful and bawdy, a place of high art and low dives, of great music and subway fiddlers. Some of the world's most notable writers have lived here: Alice B. Toklas, Robert Frost, Jack London, Kathleen Norris, and Irving Stone were born in the city. Mark Twain, William Saroyan, and John Steinbeck wrote here. Amy Tan, Danielle Steel, Dave Eggers, and Thomas Sanchez still do. Old San Franciscans like to note that Caruso sang in San Francisco the night before the '06 quake and fire and that Jack London covered the disaster for a New York magazine. The first part of the century was, in fact, a golden era for the arts in San Francisco. Among the city's writers were novelist Gertrude Atherton; literary pioneer Mary Austin; Gelett Burgess, who wrote the doggerel poem "The Purple Cow"; poet Yone Noguchi; Ambrose Bierce, a bitter man of letters who wrote a column in the *Examiner*; Sinclair Lewis, who lived in San Francisco briefly but was fired from his newspaper job for incompetence; and George Sterling, the city's unoffi-

The writer Ambrose Bierce (top), the poet George Sterling (in leopard skin), and novelist Jack London (with his boat the *Snark* under construction) flourished in San Francisco around the time of the 1906 fire and earthquake.

cial poet laureate in 1915. An admirer of wine, women, song, and opium, Sterling killed himself in his rooms at the Bohemian Club in San Francisco in 1926 after he was replaced as toastmaster at a banquet honoring H.L. Mencken. Sterling burned his last poem, which spoke of "the darkness still beyond."

In the '20s, Samuel Dashiell Hammett lived in San Francisco, worked as a private eye in the Flood Building, and wrote masterful detective stories. His most famous, *The Maltese Falcon*, was set in the dark and rainy San Francisco of December 1928, a setting, he said, that was "as real as a dime." Hammett moved away, and San Francisco's literary tide went out, but not for long. In the '30s, new writers arrived. "I once knew the city very well," John Steinbeck wrote, "spent my attic days there." William Saroyan created his first major story, "The Daring Young Man on the Flying Trapeze," at 348 Carl Street, between the N streetcar tracks and Kezar Stadium. His heart was in Fresno, but he loved San Francisco ("every block is a short story, every hill a novel"). His 1939 Pulitzer Prize-winning play *The Time of Your Life* was set in a San Francisco saloon.

At left: Dashiell Hammett and daughter Mary on the roof of the apartment building on Eddy Street where the family lived in the 1920s while he was writing his first detective stories. Gertrude Atherton (with her dog in Pacific Heights, above), John Steinbeck (at right), and William Saroyan made San Francisco a character in their books. Steinbeck always called it "The City."

Among the figures of the San Francisco Renaissance, also known as the Beat Generation, were Lawrence Ferlinghetti (above), who founded the City Lights bookstore; poet Bob Kaufman (left), who co-founded *Beatitude* magazine; and Michael McClure, one of the poets at the famous Six Gallery reading in 1955. The center of their world was North Beach.

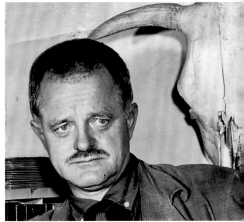

Life was tough during the Depression, but the arts flourished. Diego Rivera, the Mexican muralist, came to San Francisco in the '30s and painted noted murals at the California School of Fine Arts (now the San Francisco Art Institute) on Russian Hill, at City College, and in what is now the City Club. Rivera also had a major influence on public art, particularly on muralists such as Victor Arnautoff, Rinaldo Cuneo, Bernard Zakheim, and Robert Howard, who painted the murals inside Coit Tower, as well as Anton Refregier, who created the murals in the Rincon Annex post office. Their works were examples of social realism and were controversial in their day. The California School of Fine Arts was a wellspring of creative activity in the '30s, '40s, and '50s. On its faculty at one time or another were photographers Ansel Adams, Imogen Cunningham, and Dorothea Lange. So were painters David Park, Elmer Bischoff, and Richard Diebenkorn, who inspired the Bay Area figurative school of painting. Benny Bufano, who came to San Francisco from Italy via New York in 1914, was one of a kind. His sculptures, big and small, of cats, horses, sea lions, saints, and heroes, are still to be found all over the

On an October night in 1955, at a poetry reading by five poets at Six Gallery on Fillmore Street, Allen Ginsberg (above left) read his poem "Howl" aloud for the first time in public. Gary Snyder (top), another participant, later called the occasion "a curious kind of turning point in American poetry." Poet Kenneth Rexroth (above) was the master of ceremonies. Afterward, Lawrence Ferlinghetti wired Ginsberg: "I greet you at the beginning of a great career." Ferlinghetti was prosecuted for publishing and selling copies of the poem but was cleared in 1957.

San Francisco writers of a more recent vintage include Armistead Maupin (far right), whose *Tales of the City* began as a serial in *The Chronicle*. He went on to write a number of successful books about life in San Francisco.

At top: Po Bronson, who wrote several best-sellers, worked on one of them in a closet at The Grotto, the Market Street writers' co-op he helped to found. The co-op later moved to a former dog and cat hospital on Fell Street.

At right: David Eggers, author of *A Heartbreaking Work of Staggering Genius* and *You Shall Know Our Velocity*, also founded 826 Valencia, a Mission district writing lab for youths thirteen to eighteen. Opposite: Herb Caen wrote a daily newspaper column for fifty-eight years, longer than anyone. He also produced eleven books. On his eightieth birthday, he celebrates with his favorite drink, Vitamin V (for vodka).

Opposite, below: Novelist Amy Tan (at left) is most famous for *The Joy Luck Club*, which was a best-seller and was made into a movie. Danielle Steel, author of romantic fantasies, might be San Francisco's most prolific author.

city. Among his favorite subjects: Sun Yat-sen and St. Francis of Assisi.

After World War II, the Beat Generation writers and poets were drawn, as poet Lawrence Ferlinghetti said, to a city that was "very much a place where the West ended." Among them: Jack Kerouac, Gary Snyder, Neal Cassady, Michael McClure, Philip Whelan, Kenneth Rexroth, Bob Kaufman, Kenneth Patchen, Allen Ginsberg, and William Everson, also known as Brother Antoninus. They came to San Francisco, the *New Yorker* said, "to get out in the open, in order to breathe fresh, creative air." But they hung out on upper Grant Avenue, at places like the Co-Existence Bagel Shop, where the air was thick with tobacco and marijuana smoke, or The Cellar, where poets jammed with beboppers and bongos. The area around City Lights bookstore at Broadway and Columbus was ground zero of a small universe. In the late '50s and early '60s, Johnny Mathis was singing at Ann's 440 Club, Lenny Bruce was doing standup at the Off Broadway, Phyllis Diller and the Smothers Brothers were telling jokes at the Purple Onion, and Jonathan Winters was making people laugh at the hungry i (for "intellectual"). Hungry i owner

World-renowned
San Francisco photographers
Imogen Cunningham (above),
Dorothea Lange (with tripod),
and Ansel Adams worked
in San Francisco at the same
time and knew each other well.
Cunningham is shown near the
end of her life, Lange while she
was photographing people
during the Depression, and
Adams in his beloved Yosemite.

Enrico Banducci booked a young Barbra Streisand in 1963 at $450 a week as the opening act for a little-known standup comedian named Woody Allen, and the club reportedly did terrible business all week. Other rising stars worked there — Mort Sahl, Bill Cosby, Bob Newhart, and the Kingston Trio.

By 1966, the era of sex, drugs, and rock and roll had dawned in the Haight-Ashbury. Fueled by the psychedelic drug LSD, a youth revolution was in the works. More than a thousand long-haired, strange-looking young people in Salvation Army castoffs turned up for "A Tribute to Dr. Strange," the first acid rock dance/concert, at the Longshoreman's Hall in October 1965. By January 1967, the Human Be-In in Golden Gate Park drew ten thousand to hear music and poetry, smoke dope, and listen to LSD guru Timothy Leary tell them to "turn on, tune in, and drop out." The psychedelic rock scene bloomed. The Jefferson Airplane first played at a club called the Matrix on Fillmore Street in the Marina; the first managers of the Airplane were copyboys at *The Chronicle*. A former jug band out of Palo Alto called the Warlocks — soon to change its name to the Grateful Dead — became the house band for a series of events dubbed Acid

Above left: Eccentric sculptor Benny Bufano with one of his larger works — *Hand of Peace* — at Kearny and Market streets as the piece is moved to Fox Plaza in 1966. Above : Painter Richard Diebenkorn, shown with his *Landscape #3* and *Chair Outside*, was one of the founders of the Bay Area figurative movement.

A tremendous entertainment scene blossomed in North Beach in the '50s and early '60s. Enrico Banducci (in the beret at right), owner of the hungry i nightclub, was the impresario of the scene. He helped launch the careers of such future stars as (clockwise from top) the Kingston Trio (with comedian Ronnie Schell and his guitar) and comedians Phyllis Diller, Bill Cosby, Mort Sahl, and Jonathan Winters.
Opposite: Many young entertainers also played the Purple Onion nightclub, a rival of the hungry i.

Tests run by renegade novelist Ken Kesey and his group of psychedelic warriors called the Merry Pranksters. All the bands sported funny names — Big Brother and the Holding Company (featuring Texas transplant Janis Joplin on incendiary vocals), Quicksilver Messenger Service, Sopwith Camel, Moby Grape, and Country Joe and the Fish. The hippies danced every weekend underneath colorful light shows at the Avalon Ballroom and the Fillmore Auditorium, where impresario Bill Graham launched his fabled career. San Francisco was the music capital of the world as new groups like Santana, Creedence Clearwater Revival, and Sly and the Family Stone emerged almost daily, it seemed, from the underground.

The city had a long tradition of music and dancing in the streets that went back to the Gold Rush and the Barbary Coast, an area of crime, vice, violence — and excitement. The Coast had been destroyed in the 1906 fire but soon was rebuilt along Pacific Street. "We called it 'Terrific Street' ... you could see the lights for miles," said Sid LeProtti, a musician and later bandleader at Purcell's, an African American club where Al Jolson learned to dance the Texas Tommy and New Orleans jazzman King

The jazz scene: Lu Watters (at near right) at the Dawn Club in the late 1940s and the great bassist Vernon Alley (at far right) in 1976. Below: Jazz great Dexter Gordon adjusts his reed during a set at a San Francisco club on January 9, 1961.

Oliver played his trumpet. Purcell's had taxi dancers (twenty cents a dance) who could be persuaded to

do grander things for more money. At Purcell's, "a visitor either drank and drank frequently or was

thrown into the street," according to Herbert Asbury in his book, *The Barbary Coast*. Before he com-

posed *The Grand Canyon Suite*, Ferdinand Grofé was the house pianist at the Hippodrome, and

Art Hickman led one of the first big band jazz orchestras in the country at the St. Francis Hotel before

the First World War. Bandleader Paul Whiteman began his career at the Fairmont Hotel. LeProtti

claimed that the word "jazz" first appeared in print in the *San Francisco Bulletin* in 1913. And there was

jazz aplenty in the Barbary Coast. Among the musicians was Jelly Roll Morton, who owned a dance hall

there before World War I. The Coast was too rowdy for modern-day San Francisco, and reformers shut

it down in 1921, but LeProtti and his band went on for years.

In 1940, white musicians, notably Lu (for Lucius) Watters, took up traditional jazz — the old

razzamatazz Dixieland — at the Dawn Club in an alley near the Palace Hotel. They developed anoth-

The audience at a Beatles concert at the Cow Palace in August 1964 screamed so loud, it was said, that nobody could hear the music. Above right: One of the most famous groups in the San Francisco sound, the Grateful Dead pose at Haight and Ashbury streets in May 1974.

er San Francisco sound with, among others, Turk Murphy and Bob Scobey and his Frisco Jazz Band. Vernon Alley, a black musician who died in 2004 at the age of eighty-nine, left his hometown to tour with the Lionel Hampton and Count Basie orchestras, but soon he returned to spend his long life playing jazz in the city he loved.

Jazz always flourished in San Francisco. The Club Hangover on the side of Nob Hill, where Louis Armstrong once staged a historic benefit for ailing clarinetist Pee Wee Russell, featured on successive weeks Red Nichols, Jack Teagarden, Muggsy Spanier, Kid Ory, and George Lewis. All the greats came to play at the Blackhawk in the Tenderloin, the Jazz Workshop on Broadway, and Jimbo's Bop City in the Fillmore, where Armstrong once saw Charlie Parker play and an underage Oakland high school kid named Clint Eastwood used to sneak in. A Chinese club scene, built around such places as the Forbidden City on Sutter Street and the Shanghai Low in Chinatown, ran for nearly twenty years. All the famous old-fashioned show business greats — from Sammy Davis Jr. to Nat King Cole, from

Janis Joplin of Port Arthur, Texas, came to San Francisco in the unforgettable '60s and became the singer in a new rock group, Big Brother and the Holding Company.

Below: The psychedelic rock band the Jefferson Airplane made its debut in San Francisco in 1965, and the group was joined a year later by vocalist Grace Slick (bottom). Later the band morphed into the Jefferson Starship (below, from left: Aynsley Dunbar, David Freiberg, Mickey Thomas, Craig Chaquico, Pete Sears, and Paul Kantner) and then just Starship.

Dancers share the spotlight at the last performance of The Band at Winterland on November 25, 1976. Among those on stage that night: Bob Dylan, Ringo Starr, Neil Diamond, Joni Mitchell, Neil Young, and Van Morrison. Winterland, an old ice arena, was turned into a concert hall by rock impresario Bill Graham, shown at right on his property high in the Marin hills in 1985.

Duke Ellington to Marlene Dietrich — played the Fairmont Hotel's elegant supper club, the Venetian Room. The nightclub scene changed with the rise of rock, and modern-day rock stars such as Huey Lewis and the News, Journey, Metallica, and Chris Isaak came out of small San Francisco clubs. Over a century, the music has never stopped.

Great Performances

As the city rebuilt from the ruins of 1906, its residents returned to their passion for classical music. San Francisco was unique among American cities because it offered not only European grand opera but Chinese opera as well. Though the city's theaters and the Tivoli Opera House were casualties of the 1906 disaster, it was not long before opera returned to San Francisco, and by the early '20s, there was serious talk of forming a San Francisco opera company. Gaetano Merola, conductor of the touring San Carlo Opera, came to San Francisco often. In 1923, the San Francisco Opera was formally incorporated un-

Above left: Songwriter Tom Waits, in front of the New Mission Theater at Twenty-second and Mission streets, has been writing and performing for more than thirty years. *Real Gone* in 2004 was his fourth album in five years. His records sell only modestly, but big names like Bruce Springsteen, Rod Stewart, and the Eagles have performed his songs. Above: Carlos Santana was raised in Mexico and moved with his family to San Francisco's Mission district in 1961. His driving Latin beat caught on: he has made dozens of albums and was inducted into the Rock and Roll Hall of Fame in 1998. Here he performs at the all-star tribute to Jimi Hendrix at the Warfield Theater in 2004.

San Franciscans have always loved opera, and Italian opera star Luisa Tetrazzini, the most famous diva of her day, loved San Francisco. Wearing a huge hat, she performs above in 1912 in one of her several free concerts at Lotta's Fountain at Kearny, Geary and Market streets. **Opposite, top: The San Francisco Opera performs a scene from Act III of** *Saint François d'Assise.*

der Merola's direction, presenting its first work, *La Boheme,* in the Civic Auditorium. In a great leap of faith, the company moved into the new War Memorial Opera House in the Civic Center in 1932, the very depths of the Depression. A year later, *Time* magazine called the building "the finest opera house in the U.S." Merola *was* the Opera until his death in 1953. When Kurt Herbert Adler took over, he said, "I inherited a city uniquely devoted to opera." True enough. Among the landmarks of the first fifty years were the American debut of Renata Tebaldi and Mario del Monaco in *Aïda* (1950) and the U.S. debuts of Elisabeth Schwarzkopf (1955) and Birgit Nilsson in *Die Walküre* (1956).

Adler was succeeded by Terence McEwen in 1981, and Lotfi Mansouri took over in 1988. Mansouri produced a number of new and innovative operas, including *Dangerous Liaisons, Harvey Milk, A Streetcar Named Desire,* and *Dead Man Walking.* After Mansouri, in 2001, came Pamela Rosenberg, American-born director of the Stuttgart Opera, who promised a different vision — including new and more challenging works. She staged seldom-performed works by Shostakovich and Janacek as well as Messi-

Kurt Herbert Adler (far left) was general manager of the San Francisco Opera for twenty-eight years; Terence McEwen (above, left) directed the Opera in the '80s; Lotfi Mansouri (above), was director in the '90s; and Pamela Rosenberg brought the company into the twenty-first century.

Pierre Monteux was the
famously popular conductor
of the San Francisco Symphony
in the 1930s and '40s.
At right: Gaetano Merola
conducts the San Francisco
Opera orchestra at Stern Grove
on August 30, 1953. While
conducting the concert,
Merola collapsed and died
of a heart attack.

aen's stunning *Saint François d'Assise*. But the economy turned bad soon after Rosenberg arrived, and

the Opera had to scale back. Budgets were cut, productions canceled, and in 2004, with the Opera run-

ning a $3.8 million deficit, she announced she would leave when her contract expired in 2006. David

Gockley, longtime head of the Houston Grand Opera, was named new general director.

Another major cultural group, the San Francisco Symphony, gave its first concert in 1911 under the

baton of Henry Hadley, a distinguished composer. He was succeeded in 1915 by Alfred Hertz, who con-

ducted the opera orchestra the night Caruso sang *Carmen*. Hertz was the conductor when violinist

Yehudi Menuhin, then a local seven-year-old prodigy, made his debut with the San Francisco Sym-

phony in 1923. Hertz, who retired in 1930, was replaced by Pierre Monteux, a music legend who had

conducted the first performance of Stravinsky's *Rite of Spring* in Paris in 1913 — a feat greeted by boos

and catcalls from the audience. San Franciscans warmly received Monteux, a master of music who al-

so was a town character, an elderly man with a white mustache, walking his dog on Nob Hill. Other

At top: Seiji Ozawa conducted the Symphony for many years. Above: Violinist Yehudi Menuhin, who made his debut in the city as a child prodigy, came back in 1997 to receive an honorary degree from San Francisco State University.

maestros were Enrique Jorda, Josef Krips, Seiji Ozawa, Edo de Waart, and Herbert Blomstedt, whose

tenure lasted ten years and who led the orchestra on five trips to Europe and three to Asia. Among the

guest conductors was Michael Tilson Thomas, who led the orchestra in Gustav Mahler's Ninth Sym-

phony when he was twenty-nine. In 1995, Thomas, by then one of the world's leading interpreters of

Mahler, signed on as the Symphony's conductor and music director. Thomas — who goes by the ini-

tials "MTT" — has been a major force in the city's cultural life.

San Francisco's ballet company was the first professional classical ballet company in the United States.

It began in 1933 as the San Francisco Opera Ballet, and its purpose then was to train dancers to appear in

opera productions. In 1938, Willam Christensen, one of three brothers — the others were Harold, who

ran the ballet school, and Lew, a dancer and then the company's director — came to San Francisco and

the Opera Ballet. In 1939, Willam choreographed *Coppelia*, the company's first full-length production. In

1942, Willam and Harold purchased the Opera Ballet for eight hundred dollars and renamed it the

Michael Tilson Thomas, a brilliant musician and expert on Gustav Mahler, is not only the Symphony conductor but also a San Francisco celebrity. He poses at his home on his sixtieth birthday in 2004.

San Francisco Ballet. On Christmas Eve 1944, Willam presented the American premiere of *The Nut-cracker*. Lew took over the company in 1952 and choreographed more than one hundred productions, including *The Nutcracker*. Lew, who made Michael Smuin his co-director and heir apparent, died in 1984. That year, the Ballet board made a startling decision. Smuin was shown the door, and retiring New York City Ballet principal dancer Helgi Tomasson was made the company's artistic director. Tomasson has reigned for more than twenty years. The company that the Christensens bought now has an international reputation, like the Opera and Symphony. Critic Clive Barnes said it "now stands in that major league once consisting of the New York City Ballet and the American Ballet Theatre."

San Francisco has been a theater town since the Gold Rush and in early 1906 had eight downtown theaters. Not only did Caruso sing in San Francisco on the eve of the earthquake, but John Barrymore also appeared on stage. The ashes had barely cooled from the great fire before San Franciscans began attending shows again. Temporary theaters opened in the unburned Western Addition, and by 1911, downtown San

Willam Christensen, a Ballet pioneer, teaches a class toward the end of his career in 1992. Above, right: Director Michael Smuin watches dancers perform *Les Noces* at the San Francisco Academy Ballet in 1999. After leaving the San Francisco Ballet, Smuin went on to form his own highly successful company, Smuin Ballet.
Below right: Yuan Yuan Tan and Gonzalo Garcia perform *Apollo* in the Ballet's 2004 season.

Helgi Tomasson, the
San Francisco Ballet's artistic
director, and ballerina
Elizabeth Loscavio talk things
over at a rehearsal in 1991.

Francisco once more could boast of eight theaters, offering everything from vaudeville and musical com-

edy to serious drama. The oldest surviving theater is the Geary, which opened in January 1910 and ever

since has remained at the heart of the city's legitimate stage scene. The '20s were boom times for the stage

in San Francisco. Three large theaters — the Curran, the Golden Gate, and the Warfield — opened in

1922. All three are still going. The Curran was named for impresario Homer Curran, who got Sam and

Lee Shubert in New York to help finance his eight-hundred-thousand-dollar showplace. When that deal

ended in 1939, Curran organized the San Francisco Civic Light Opera and made an arrangement with a

similar organization in Los Angeles to produce "top-rate dramatic entertainment" on the West Coast.

Immediately before and after World War II, the San Francisco stage glittered with stars — Edward

G. Robinson, Basil Rathbone, Frederic March, Ethel Barrymore, Paul Muni, Paul Robeson, Cornelia

Otis Skinner, and Judith Anderson appeared at the Geary. The Curran hosted Eddie Foy, Gertrude

Lawrence, Tallulah Bankhead, Katharine Hepburn, Vincent Price, and native daughter Carol Chan-

Opposite: Ellen McLaughlin appears in the Pulitizer Prize-winning drama *Angels in America* at the Eureka Theater. Top left: Robin Williams in drag on a cable car in the film *Mrs. Doubtfire*. Top center: Michael Douglas and Karl Malden, near Alcatraz, starred in the television series *Streets of San Francisco*. At left: James Stewart rescues Kim Novak from the bay in Alfred Hitchcock's *Vertigo*. Above: Clint Eastwood as *Dirty Harry*, the renegade San Francisco movie cop.

ning. In the 1950s, San Francisco developed a strong regional theater. Jules Irving and Herbert Blau, two San Francisco State College professors, organized the Actor's Workshop, which became one of the country's major regional companies. San Francisco theater suffered a blow when Irving and Blau moved to New York in 1965, but they were replaced by the American Conservatory Theater, which moved from Pittsburgh. ACT opened its first San Francisco season at the Geary in 1967 and became one of the country's premier theater companies.

In the meantime, San Francisco was on the cutting edge of innovative theater. The Magic Theater premiered works by Sam Shepard, including *Buried Child* (1978) and *True West* (1980). The new Eureka Theater premiered *Angels in America* in 1991. *Buried Child* and *Angels in America* won Pulitzer Prizes for drama. Not all theater was staged inside: In 1959, R.G. Davis founded the San Francisco Mime Troupe, which brought its own kind of politically inspired drama to the city's streets and parks. It was theater without the theater.

Clockwise from above: Film director and actress Joan Chen; madam Sally Stanford in 1952, later mayor of Sausalito; Russ Hodges and Lon Simmons, first radio voices of the San Francisco Giants; exercise guru Jack LaLanne on his ninetieth birthday in 2004.

Players on the City's Stage

Whether they were born here or adopted the city as their own, creative and colorful people made an impression during the San Francisco Century. An incomplete list:

Stewart Brand, producer of *The Whole Earth Catalogue* ... sculptor **Ruth Asawa** ... street mime **Robert Shields** ... **Ina Coolbrith**, poet laureate of California ... film directors **George Lucas**, **Phil Kaufman**, and **Chris Columbus** ... **Rod McKuen**, author of *Stanyan Street and Other Sorrows* ... **Daniel Handler**, writing under the name Lemony Snicket ... **Chet Helms**, 1960s rock promoter ... **Isaac Stern**, classical violinist ... landscape architects **Lawrence Halprin** and **John McLaren**, "father" of Golden Gate Park ...**Julia Morgan**, who used wood and stone to create beauty ... **Willis Polk**, designer of the Hallidie Building ... engineer **T.Y. Lin**, influenced design of bridges and structures worldwide ... **Ben Fong Torres**, writer for **Jann Wenner**'s *Rolling Stone*, which grew out of the '60s New Left magazine *Ramparts* ... **Oakley Hall**, novelist and literary guru ... **Art Finley**,

television's "Mayor Art" … actor **Bill Irwin**, who started with Pickle Family Circus … **Charlie Low**, owner of the all-Chinese Night Club, the Forbidden City, in the '40s … **Don Sherwood**, the World's Greatest Disc Jockey in the '50s … **Alan Watts**, philosopher … artist **Robert Crumb** …Wayne **Thiebaud**, painter… **Peter Coyote**, actor … **Steve Silver**, creator of Beach Blanket Babylon … **Margo St. James**, former prostitute and advocate for sex workers' rights … **Brownie Mary**, who wanted to turn the world on, one marijuana brownie at a time … **Edsel Ford Fong**, cantankerous Chinatown waiter … **Izzy Gomez**, owner of a '30s saloon that attracted sailors, longshoremen, and drinking ladies … colorful **Henri Lenoir**, who ran the Vesuvio bar … **Trader Vic Bergeron**, father of the mai tai and owner of the restaurant where the elite met to eat … **Davey Rosenberg**, press agent who invented topless dancing in North Beach … **Francis Van Wie**, Muni man with more than a dozen wives, was called the Ding Dong Daddy of the D Car Line … **George K. Whitney**, whose Laughing Sal at his Playland-at-the-Beach was a symbol of at least a corner of San Francisco.

Clockwise from top above: Singer Johnny Mathis came back to San Francisco State College, his alma mater, in 1958 to help pick "The Most Beautiful Girl on Campus" from among these finalists; Boz Scaggs, songwriter and musician; poet and novelist Maya Angelou; director Francis Ford Coppola; comedian and actor Robin Williams; actress Carol Channing, who came from Lowell High School to belt out *Hello, Dolly!*

PART NINE

City of the Imagination

San Francisco is a city of uncommon beauty, unrivaled by any other in the country and few places in the world. On a flawless spring day, the city can take your breath away; sometimes it appears as unreal as a painted stage set. It is difficult now to imagine that San Francisco was little else but smoking ruins after the earthquake

> The city's unusual weather is evident the day after Christmas, 1999, when bright sunshine lures people to Golden Gate Park. San Francisco has as many as thirty microclimates — and conditions can be dramatically different at the same time of day in different parts of the city.

and fire of April 18, 1906. Yet, after a century, the city continues to commemorate the disaster at 5:12 a.m. every year to recognize those who died and the spirit that built a new San Francisco. Even a few survivors, very old men and women, are on hand to be honored as living symbols of the city's past.

San Francisco has a dramatic and colorful history. Surrounded on three sides by water, founded as the farthest outpost of the Spanish empire, once a little Mexican town jolted into a city by an amazing gold rush, destroyed in an earthquake and burned to the ground, San Francisco developed its own legend.

Beauty and a sort of mystical charm, hard to define, make the city special. It is on the edge of a con-

tinent, a journey's end. Americans from the other side of the Mississippi came in covered wagons, following the setting sun to the Golden West. Asians sailed east across the Pacific to the place the Chinese called "Gold Mountain." Latinos came from Mexico to *El Norte* in 1776.

As a result, San Francisco today is richly diverse: African Americans, Russians, Italians, Turks, Cambodians, Koreans, Peruvians, people talking on cell phones in a more than a dozen languages. It is a place where the phone book in 2005 had nearly three times as many people named Wong (3,003) as were named Smith (1,062).

San Francisco is a city where living is more important than making a living. It had 3,382 restaurants the last time the Convention & Visitors Bureau counted, which means San Franciscans could eat out every day for nine years and three months and never go to the same restaurant twice. The oldest restaurant, the Tadich Grill, first opened in 1849, making it older than Canada.

The city embraces new ideas and new people. It is no surprise that the bohemians at the turn of the

twentieth century found a home in San Francisco. So did the Beats, the hippies, and the dot-com in-

novators. The city always has been open to other lifestyles, which is why the gay population felt wel-

come. It is a place where people could come to disappear or to reinvent themselves. Who you were is

not as important as who you are.

San Francisco is where Philo T. Farnsworth invented television, where A.P. Giannini founded the

Bank of America. It has been the home of Levi Strauss and topless dancing. Sourdough French bread

comes from San Francisco; the first cioppino was served in the city, the first crab Louis, the first "It's It"

ice cream bar. Some say the martini was invented in San Francisco, but that might be only a legend.

San Francisco is a small town pretending to be a city. "A village, really," said writer Herb Gold.

"Everybody knows everybody." It is a city that loves to look at itself in the mirror, a town that half be-

lieves the tourist hype about America's Favorite City while looking past the panhandlers on its famous

streets. It is becoming a city where housing is so expensive the middle class can no longer afford to buy

Emilio Mercado (above) does T'ai Chi in Golden Gate Park on a sunny morning in 2001. Opposite: A stairway in the Museum of Modern Art, designed by Swiss architect Mario Botta and described by *Chronicle* architecture critic Allan Temko as having "spiritual grandeur." During the late '90s, SFMOMA made international art news with acquisitions of works by Rene Magritte, Piet Mondrian, Francis Bacon, Jasper Johns, Eva Hesse, Cy Twombly, and others. Much of the collection was made possible by trustee Phyllis Wattis, who gave millions to Bay Area arts institutions. Pages 230-231: A blossoming cherry tree in Golden Gate Park entices Alana Frost and her sons Samuel and Jerrymiah in 2005.

A quiet morning in North Beach is a great time to sip a cappuccino while reading or working on a laptop at the Caffe Trieste, said to be the first espresso coffeehouse on the West Coast. It was established at 601 Vallejo Street in 1956 by Giovanni Giotta, "Papa Gianni," who brought his family to San Francisco from Rovigno, Italy. The cafe has been a hangout for bohemian poets, Beat writers, Italians from the neighborhood, celebrities, and tourists, many of whom were entertained by Giotta family members and others performing musical numbers, from opera to show tunes.

a home. Two-thirds of San Franciscans were renters in 2005, and there were more dogs (150,000 by some estimates) than children (130,000 by the US Census).

Yet San Franciscans will tell you they would not live anywhere else. There is something beyond its beauty, its location, its lifestyle. Something in the air — maybe the bright light of spring and of October, when the city seems to glisten, when the Farallon Islands stand out in the ocean at the end of the streets in the Sunset. Something different, something that veils the city like a summer mist.

What is it that makes San Francisco so special? "That's a question," wrote Herb Caen, "with one hundred answers."

The Critical Mass bike run, held the last Friday of every month during rush hour, was started in the '90s to disrupt traffic to call attention to the concerns of cyclists. Above, more than one thousand cyclists join Critical Mass in a ride down Stockton Street on August 30, 1996, welcoming bicycle messengers from around the world who came to the city to compete in the Bicycle Messenger World Championship races. At left: Surfer Steve Miller leaves Kelly's Cove at Ocean Beach after a morning surf in 2004. Pages 234-235: Everything's beautiful at the ballet as these unidentified janitors observe Anthony Randazzo and Tina LeBlanc rehearse for opening night, 1994.

Perhaps it is something in the air, but sourdough French bread has flourished in San Francisco since Isadore Boudin produced the first loaf in the fall of 1849. The Boudin bakery at Tenth and Geary bakes twenty thousand pounds of dough each day.
At right: The cable car bell-ringing contest, an annual event at Union Square, draws a crowd as Warren Robinson shows his stuff.

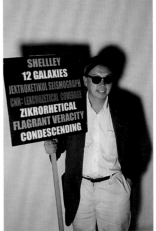

At top: Years after the Summer of Love — the Haight Ashbury Gift Shop in the Haight kicks up its heels in 2005.

Above: Frank Chu, town personality, has been warning of the dangers of the "12 Galaxies" for a number of years. He inspired the name of a music club on Mission Street called 12 Galaxies. When he started, the city was more formal, so he wore a tie every day. Now, every day is dress-down Friday.

At left: Identical twins Vivian and Marian Brown, local characters, shake a leg on Telegraph Hill, the Transamerica Pyramid towering in the distance.

Pages 238: Fog settles over the city as vacationers Wolfgang and Marion Haberkorn, their sons Jonas and Nicolas, and their goddaughter Sarah take in the view from the Marin Headlands.

City of the Imagination | 237

Two Cherry Blossom Queen candidates in the 2000 Northern California Cherry Blossom Festival stroll past cherry trees at the Japanese Peace Plaza.

At right: Passengers ride the N-Judah streetcar at Carl and Cole streets on a rainy spring day in 2001.

Opposite: Sunday brunch at the elegant Garden Court of the Palace Hotel in 2004, still an event worth dressing up for.

Pages 242-243: Only in San Francisco — In a World Series first, kayakers dressed in Santa Claus regalia wait in McCovey Cove in hopes of retrieving a home run hit out of Pacific Bell Park in game four, 2002. The Giants beat the Anaheim Angels 4-3 but lost the Series.

Another "only in San Francisco" moment — Bob Comstock sports a shower cap and towel at the twenty-fifth annual Exotic Erotic Ball, a celebration of sexuality and freedom of expression, in 2004.

At left: A dachshund's head from a former Doggie Diner restaurant was named a city landmark in 2000.

Opposite: John's Grill, an Ellis Street fixture since 1908, was the first restaurant to open downtown as the area was rebuilt after the fire of 1906. Dashiell Hammett's detective Sam Spade lunched at John's in the novel *The Maltese Falcon.*

Pages 246-247. The city skyline seen from Treasure Island at dusk shines with holiday lights beneath a crescent moon. Good night.

ACKNOWLEDGMENTS

Many people made this book possible, among them my father, William C. Nolte, who taught a little kid to appreciate his native city.

Also, Tom McGarvey, former owner of Red's Java House, who told me about the waterfront in the old days; Mike McGarvey, his brother and partner; Captain Bill Figari, who spent a lifetime on the bay; Captain Kip Carlsen and Captain Art Thomas, bar pilots who told me how to steer ships; Richard Perri, San Francisco's greatest undiscovered artist; Dennis Kennedy and his associates at the fireboats *Phoenix* and *Guardian*; Steve Canright, waterfront historian; the late Mayor George Christopher, who told me about his adventures with Nikita Khrushchev of the USSR and Horace Stoneham of the Giants; Rose Marie Cleese, who admired her grandfather, the late Mayor Angelo J. Rossi; Susan Goldstein of the San Francisco Public Library history room; Paul Kantus of the Noe Valley Archives; Howard Wong, architect; Joyce Chan of the Chinese Historical Society of America; Him Mark Lai, the foremost historian of the Chinese American experience; Mauricio Vela, neighborhood activist in the Mission and Bernal Heights; Bob Hernandez, once president of the Mission Rebels; Ron Battistoni and his wife, Rose, who grew up in the Mission; the Reverend Tom Seagrave, once pastor at St. Peter's Catholic Church; Phil Jaber, a philosopher who sells coffee one cup at a time on Twenty-fourth Street; Susan Cervantes of the Precita Eyes Project; Miguel Bustos, who loves the Mission; Strange de Jim and Ken Maley, guides to the Castro; Rich Reed, a bosun and guide to San Francisco Bay; Taren Sapienza, who organizes the 1906 earthquake commemorations; John Cantwell, Alcatraz ranger; and Jim Adams, who makes the Blue & Gold boats run on time.

Thanks to Robert Rosenthal, managing editor of *The San Francisco Chronicle*, for his idea to do this book. Other *Chronicle* staff members whose help was valuable: Michele Anderson, Jennifer Asche, David Baker, Kenneth Baker, Nanette Bisher, Joe Brown, Mark Costantini, John Curley, Victoria Elliott, Gary Fong, Leah Garchik, Carlos Avila Gonzalez, Tom Graham, Randy Greenwell, Richard Geiger, Jesse Hamlin, Ann Hill, Ken Howe, Robert Hurwitt, Michael Keiser, Joshua Kosman, Mark Lundgren, Michael Macor, Johnny Miller, Frank Mina, Bruce Perez, Suzanne Pullen, Judy Richter, Glenn Schwarz, Joel Selvin, Ceci Sutton, Michael Taylor, Todd Trumbull, Bill Van Niekerken, David Wiegand, Mike Wolgelenter, and Joshua Zucker.

Thanks also to proofreader Barbara Braasch and consultant Carla Lazzareschi and to Eden Collinsworth, Jacqueline Deval, Carol Edgar, Steve Falk, Barbra Frank, Teri Johnson, Lynn Ludlow, Christopher Scheer, and Carole Vernier. Also thanks to the staff at Sterling Publications for advice and patience: Charles Nurnberg, Rick Willet, Adria Dougherty, Andrew Martin, Yvette Wynne, Margaret LaSalle, Bette Gahres, Leigh Ann Ambrosi. And thanks to production liaisons Sally Liu at SNP Leefung and Josephine Yam at Colourscan.

Special thanks to those whose archives we tapped: Richard Monaco; Carolyn Cassady; Julie Rivett; Tricia Roush and Kirsten Tanaka at the San Francisco Performing Arts Library and Museum; Erica Nordmeier and Susan Snyder at the Bancroft Library, University of California, Berkeley; Bill Kooiman and Steve Davenport at the San Francisco Maritime National Historical Park; Patricia Akre at the San Francisco History Center, San Francisco Public Library; John Keibel at Wells Fargo Historical Services; Scott McKibben and John Gollin at the *San Francisco Examiner*; Joseph Evans at the California Historical Society; Bill McMorris of the Oakland Museum; Susan Grinols at the Fine Arts Museums of San Francisco; David Ruiz of Pacific Aerial Surveys; and the Associated Press.
— *Carl Nolte*

CREDITS

COVER: Frederic Larson, *San Francisco Chronicle*

PAGE 2: Fred Larson, *San Francisco Chronicle*

PAGE 6: Tom Levy, *San Francisco Chronicle*

CHAPTER 1 | PAGE 8: (Top) B(alfe) D. Johnson, c. 1905; Muhlman Photographic Collection; Courtesy of the San Francisco Maritime National Historic Park; A22.16,824n. (Bottom) Photo used with permission of Wells Fargo Bank, N.A.; 9157-11

PAGE 9: Wyland Stanley Collection, *San Francisco Chronicle* Archives

PAGE 10: W.E. Worden; Courtesy of the San Francisco Maritime National Historic Park; A12.30,155 P1

PAGES 12-13: Arnold Genthe, American 1869-1942; Untitled (View of fire down Sacramento Street), 1906; Gelatin silver print, image 200 x 329 mm (7 ⅞ x 12 ¹⁵⁄₁₆ in.); Fine Arts Museums of San Francisco, Museum Collection, A046248

PAGE 14: Photo used with permission of Wells Fargo Bank, N.A.; 5621.A39

PAGE 15: San Francisco History Center, San Francisco Public Library; AAA-8916

PAGES 16-17: Bear Photo; *San Francisco Chronicle* Archives

PAGE 18: *San Francisco Chronicle* Archives

PAGE 19: (Top) *San Francisco Chronicle* Archives. (Bottom) C. Mishkin; San Francisco History Center, San Francisco Public Library; AAD-0621

PAGE 20: (Top) J.B. Monaco Photo; Courtesy of Richard Monaco. (Bottom) *San Francisco Chronicle* Archives

PAGE 21: *San Francisco Chronicle* Archives

PAGES 22-23: C.P. Magagnes; San Francisco History Center, San Francisco Public Library; AAC-2892

PAGE 24: (Top) San Francisco History Center, San Francisco Public Library; AAC-3373. (Bottom) Courtesy of the Bancroft Library, University of California, Berkeley; BANC PIC 1905.05628

PAGE 25: *San Francisco Chronicle* Archives

PAGE 26: Arnold Genthe, American 1869-1942; On the Ruins (April 1906), 1906; Gelatin silver print, image: 202 x 252 mm (7 ¹⁵⁄₁₆ x 9 ¹⁵⁄₁₆ in.); Fine Arts Museums of San Francisco, Museum Purchase, James D. Phelan Bequest Fund, A021276

PAGE 27: (Left) *San Francisco Chronicle* Archives. (Right Top) Matt Draghlevich, *San Francisco Chronicle* Archives. (Right Bottom) Arnold Genthe, American 1869-1942; Untitled (Charred corpse in street amid rubble and ruin), 1906; Gelatin silver print, image: 221 x 313 mm (8 ¹¹⁄₁₆ x 12 ⁵⁄₁₆ in.); Fine Arts Museums of San Francisco, Museum Purchase, James D. Phelan Bequest Fund, A021293

PAGE 28: Bear Photo 260, *San Francisco Chronicle* Archives

PAGES 28-29: Wyland Stanley Collection; San Francisco History Center, San Francisco Public Library; AAC-3086

PAGE 29: *San Francisco Chronicle* Archives

PAGE 30: (Top) *San Francisco Chronicle* Archives. (Bottom) *San Francisco Chronicle* Archives

PAGE 31: *San Francisco Chronicle* Archives

PAGE 32: (Top) Photo used with permission of Wells Fargo Bank, N.A.; 5621.5883c. (Bottom) Weidner; San Francisco History Center, San Francisco Public Library; AAC-3036

PAGE 33: Bear Photo 215; *San Francisco Chronicle* Archives

PAGE 34: *San Francisco Chronicle* Archives

PAGE 35: Miles Bros., *San Francisco Chronicle* Archives

PAGE 36: *San Francisco Chronicle* Archives

PAGES 36-37: *San Francisco Chronicle* Archives

PAGE 37: J.B. Monaco Photo; Courtesy Richard Monaco

CHAPTER 2 | PAGE 38: Courtesy of the San Francisco Maritime National Historic Park; A12.253n

PAGE 40: *San Francisco Chronicle* Archives

PAGE 41: *San Francisco Chronicle* Archives

PAGE 42: (Top) *San Francisco Chronicle* Archives. (Bottom) *San Francisco Chronicle* Archives

PAGE 43: (Top) San Francisco History Center, San Francisco Public Library; AAD-5199. (Bottom) *San Francisco Chronicle* Archives

PAGE 44: *San Francisco Chronicle* Archives

PAGE 45: Duke Downey, *San Francisco Chronicle*

PAGE 46: *San Francisco Chronicle* Archives

PAGE 47: Associated Press

PAGE 48: (Left) *San Francisco Chronicle* Archives

PAGES 48-49: Clem Albers, *San Francisco Chronicle*

PAGE 50: (Top) Associated Press. (Bottom) Brant Ward, *San Francisco Chronicle*

PAGE 51: Gina Gayle, *San Francisco Chronicle*

PAGE 52: Carlos Avila Gonzalez, *San Francisco Chronicle*

PAGE 53: Mike Kepka, *San Francisco Chronicle*

PAGES 54-55: Lance Iversen, *San Francisco Chronicle*

PAGE 56: (Top) Chris Stewart, *San Francisco Chronicle*. (Bottom) Frederic Larson, *San Francisco Chronicle*

PAGE 57: Lance Iversen, *San Francisco Chronicle*

CHAPTER 3 | PAGE 58: *San Francisco Chronicle* Archives

PAGE 60: San Francisco History Center, San Francisco Public Library; AAB-9559

PAGE 61: (Top) Noe Valley Archives. (Bottom) Noe Valley Archives

PAGES 62-63: Noe Valley Archives

PAGE 64: (Top) Michael Macor, *San Francisco Chronicle*. (Bottom) Chris Hardy, *San Francisco Chronicle*

PAGE 65: Michael Macor, *San Francisco Chronicle*

PAGE 66: (Top) Shades of the Mission Collection; San Francisco History Center, San Francisco Public Library; 002-634. (Bottom) FN-19825

PAGE 67: *San Francisco Chronicle* Archives

PAGE 68: Peter Da Silva, *San Francisco Chronicle*

PAGE 69: (Left) Robin Weiner, *San Francisco Chronicle*. (Right) Michael Maloney, *San Francisco Chronicle*

PAGE 70: (Left) Robin Weiner, *San Francisco Chronicle*. (Right) Carlos Avila Gonzalez, *San Francisco Chronicle*

PAGE 71: (Top) Justin Sullivan, *San Francisco Chronicle*. (Bottom) Deanne Fitzmaurice, *San Francisco Chronicle*

PAGE 72: (Top) Scott Sommerdorf, *San Francisco Chronicle*. (Bottom) Christina Koci Hernandez, *San Francisco Chronicle*

PAGE 73: Darryl Bush, *San Francisco Chronicle*

PAGES 74-75: Liz Mangelsdorf, *San Francisco Chronicle*

PAGE 76: Michael Macor, *San Francisco Chronicle*

PAGE 77: (Top) Gary Fong, *San Francisco Chronicle*. (Bottom) Kendra Luck, *San Francisco Chronicle*

PAGE 78: (Top) Liz Hafalia, *San Francisco Chronicle*. (Bottom) Gary Fong, *San Francisco Chronicle*

PAGE 79: Mike Kepka, *San Francisco Chronicle*

PAGE 80: (Both) Michael Macor, *San Francisco Chronicle*.

PAGE 81: Chris Hardy, *San Francisco Chronicle*

PAGES 82-83: Frederic Larson, *San Francisco Chronicle*

CHAPTER 4 | PAGE 84: California Historical Society; FN-31285

PAGE 86: California Historical Society; FN-22912

PAGE 87: (Top) California Historical Society; FN-10744. (Bottom) California Historical Society; FN-04899

PAGES 88-89: California Historical Society; FN-08622

PAGE 90: (Top) James Wong Howe, 1944; Courtesy of the Bancroft Library, University of California, Berkeley; BANC PIC 1996.014:7. (Bottom left) James Wong Howe, 1944; Courtesy of the Bancroft Library, University of California, Berkeley; BANC PIC 1996.014:28. (Bottom right) James Wong Howe, 1944; Courtesy of the Bancroft Library, University of California, Berkeley; BANC PIC 1996.014:21

INDEX

Note: maps are designated by the letter m; photographs are designated by page numbers in italics.

© R. Crumb